PRAISE FOR *ANIMAL WISDOM*

"This is an excellent book—it is substantive and non-sentimental, a good read, and a delightful one. Join a bigger world—include the animals in all our decision-making. Read this book. The animals are grateful for this book; you will be too."
—Matthew Fox, coauthor of *Occupy Spirituality*

"A compelling body of evidence suggests that human minds can connect with one another across space and time, but also with other sentient creatures as well. Dr. Linda Bender takes us inside these primordial connections and shows how they work toward our welfare and survival."
—Larry Dossey, MD, author of *One Mind: How Our Individual Mind Is Part of a Greater Consciousness and Why it Matters*

"There is one natural law for all of us to live by, and that is caring and sharing and being responsible for the wellbeing of all other living things. In *Animal Wisdom*, Linda Bender gives us all a chance to go back to the way that will maintain everything we have. She helps us remember what the animals have not forgotten, that we are all connected, and that no one being is less than or greater than another. Bender explains what my people have always known, that having a good relationship with all life is the key to physical, mental, social, and spiritual harmony. This is the way it was meant to be. This is the key to our survival."
—Tjilpi Bob Randall, Yankunytjatjara elder, author of *Songman: The Story of an Aboriginal Elder of Uluru*

ANIMAL
WISDOM

Dear Faith,
Thank you for the
profound love, companion and
joy you have offend to so many
animals and the people who
serve! thanks for your "giving heart"...
Love,
Linda
Bender

ANIMAL WISDOM

Learning from the Spiritual Lives of Animals

LINDA BENDER, DVM

North Atlantic Books
Berkeley, California

"The Grapes of My Body" by Rumi, originally published in *The Hope* and reprinted by permission of Hay House. Excerpt from "Who Says Words With My Mouth" by Rumi, originally published in *The Essential Rumi* and reprinted by permission of the translator.

Published by
North Atlantic Books
P.O. Box 12327
Berkeley, California 94712

Cover photo by Carolyn Evans of PhoDographer
Cover and book design by Mary Ann Casler
Printed in the United States of America

Animal Wisdom: Learning from the Spiritual Lives of Animals is sponsored by the Society for the Study of Native Arts and Sciences, a nonprofit educational corporation whose goals are to develop an educational and cross-cultural perspective linking various scientific, social, and artistic fields; to nurture a holistic view of arts, sciences, humanities, and healing; and to publish and distribute literature on the relationship of mind, body, and nature.

North Atlantic Books' publications are available through most bookstores. For further information, visit our website at www.northatlanticbooks.com or call 800-733-3000.

Library of Congress Cataloging-in-Publication Data
Bender, Linda
Animal wisdom : learning from the spiritual lives of animals / Linda Bender, DVM.
      pages cm
ISBN 978-1-58394-773-9—ISBN 978-1-58394-786-9
1. Human-animal relationships. 2. Human-animal communication. 3. Animal psychology. 4. Emotions in animals. 5. Wisdom. 6. Spiritual life. 7. Love. I. Title.
QL85.B45 2014
591.5—dc23   2013023673

2 3 4 5 6 7 8 9 Malloy 19 18 17 16 15 14

Printed on recycled paper

For—

    All the beloved creatures

    Teach us, Great Spirit,
    To walk the soft earth
    As relatives of all that live.

    —Lakota prayer

Acknowledgments

In my experience, the language of the heart often defies expression in words, and since *Animal Wisdom* is, in essence, all about the heart, bringing it to life exhausted my abilities consistently. I offer heartfelt thanks to the many human and nonhuman souls who made this work possible.

First and foremost, I thank the animals who, throughout my life, have been and continue to be my sacred teachers. In humble gratitude I bow to the buffalo in Kruger Park, South Africa, for compelling me to share "the wisdom" with the human community.

Infinite gratitude to:

> Most of all, Dad, "Nature Girl" thanks you for believing in me and my love for animals, and for your unconditional love—the best in me is because of you. I wish you were here to see the book.
>
> Tom, "Dr. Grit," whose love offered me space to dedicate myself to animal advocacy.
>
> Jamee and Nicholas for your encouragement and support— love you all the way to Heaven and back.
>
> Pepper, my beloved companion, for enriching our lives with your love, and staying by my side during the writing of the book.

A huge thank you to:

Everyone at North Atlantic Books and Random House for taking me on, and for guiding me through the publishing process.

Andrew Harvey, whose passion for sacred activism is boundless. Thank you for introducing this work to my publishers and for your wisdom, encouragement, and unfailing support over the years.

Catherine MacCoun, my friend, without your help the book would not be birthed.

Victor Paruta, thank you for setting the stage.

Rupert Sheldrake for your inspiring research, brilliant mind, and helpful suggestions.

David Simon for encouragement and hilarious animal stories. We miss you.

Deepak Chopra, master teacher.

Linda Tucker and Jason Turner, for your courage, love, and sacred action.

I would also like to acknowledge with gratitude: "Uncle" Bob Randall and Barbara Schacht Randall, the San people of the Kalahari Desert, South Africa, Carolyn Rivers, founder and director of The Sophia Institute, Carolyn Evans of PhoDographer, Trudy Twigg and Larry Stone, Jennifer and Brian Welham, Susan Rawlings, Nathan Schwartz-Salant, Gail Larson, Joel Mellon, Barb Shafer, Jill Mangino, Jill Angelo, and Bill Rogers, DVM.

TABLE OF CONTENTS

FOREWORD

It's said that nothing focuses the mind like staring down the barrel of a gun. When Linda Bender describes being held at gunpoint for about a half hour, the life memory that came back to her at that critical moment was one of reliving an experience of absolute freedom with her horse, Je t'aime, galloping bareback, in blissful union under the African skies. An expanded moment, "which swelled with God's love until a minute became forever." It is not, as you might first imagine, a moment of escapism, a transcendent and out-of-body experience, but the reverse: she was totally present and, as she put it, "in my body." There is all the difference in the world between these two conditions: the first, escaping responsibilities of earthly life, and the second, becoming fully embodied, real, and truly alive. Because when you are truly alive, you do not fear death. You do not fear anything.

If you're one of those people who dearly wishes to make a meaningful difference in our challenging world, and are hesitating simply because you haven't stepped into your truth and courage yet, then this book will be an inspiration to you from the first word to the last, including stories that are likely to bring you to tears.

Animal Wisdom is a work of pure unconditional love, not only for the animals who have shared so much of their wisdom in its pages, but also for us, mere humans, whose destiny depends on our urgently renegotiating our relationship with Mother Nature, if our species stands a chance of survival in the near future.

The profound nature of our connection with animals is presented with such tenderness and scientific authority that it would take only the most ignorant of brutes to ignore Nature's self-sacrificing call.

What makes this read so painful in parts is that the terms "brutish" and "ignorant" are understatements when it comes to describing the mess we humans find ourselves in.

At this crucial hour in the sustainability of our planet, let's face it—we are all staring down the barrel of a gun. Working on the timeless premise that love is the ultimate truth at the heart of creation has enabled Linda Bender not only to acknowledge the exploitative disease of modern consumerism that is killing us all but, more importantly, elucidate the solution.

Her light, intimate touch and heightened perspective, despite the seriousness of her subject matter, carry us at a page-turning pace right to the quintessence: how did we lose our place in Paradise, and how do we get it back?

Not by escaping from this human-made devastation we've all had a part in fabricating but simply by helping to restore Mother Nature are we finding our own true natures again. Yes, by becoming truly alive and responsible for life again, we are reclaiming hearts and souls that we've all but lost along the way.

Through one fascinating example after another, *Animal Wisdom* shows us that renewing our communication with animals is our most powerful tool to reestablishing a loving and meaningful relationship with the real world. While this ability dates back to the most ancient times, it is critically relevant to our modern day, and the key not only to protecting our planet but to saving ourselves. Linda Bender reminds us also that *anima,* the root word of animal, means "soul," so our reconnection with animals is truly a lifeline to renew our own hearts and souls—and so much else, by way of life, love, responsibility for our actions, and restoration of our environment, that will flow as a consequence.

Just as it takes us to the very heart of the matter, so this courageous book delivers us effortlessly right into the midst of those places and those issues we most dread—like what it means to die, or to lose a loved one, or what it really means to kill and eat another animal, and how differently nature's predators treat this God-given contract.

Only in the last chapter of this gripping and impeccably argued book, when her reader is openhearted enough to really listen, does Linda Bender venture to share with us some of the messages conveyed to her by animal ambassadors, including the timeless wisdom she received from the king of all animals, the magnificent white lions.

Since I myself am lucky enough to live in the wild among lions, and the white lions in particular, in the middle of their ancestral endemic pridelands of the greater Timbavati region, I can attest to the authenticity of this commanding message. While it rings with the distinct regal quality of the *king of the king of beasts,* this is the same loving and urgent imperative you will receive from any animal you are fortunate enough to encounter in your life, whether domestic or untamed, if you only pause to listen. It is a sacred message, a plea from the heart and soul of Mother Nature and the Creative Force behind all Her creatures great and small, wise and wonderful.

Only by heeding their call can we begin to restore Paradise on Earth.

—Linda Tucker
CEO, Global White Lion Protection Trust and
author of *Saving the White Lions* and *Mystery of the White Lions*

PART ONE

The Fabric of Creation

Chapter 1

THE ECOLOGY OF PARADISE

And while I still have much to learn, this much I know: animals are indeed more ancient, more complex, and in many ways more sophisticated than us. They are more perfect because they remain within Nature's fearful symmetry just as Nature intended. They should be respected and revered, and perhaps none more so than the elephant, the world's most emotionally human land mammal.

—DAPHNE SHELDRICK

One does not meet oneself until one catches the reflection from an eye other than human.

—LOREN EISELEY

As a child, I was awkward, shy, and slow to learn to talk. I had trouble connecting with other people and seeing how I fit in with the world around me. When I look back on the first six years of my life, I can't remember much. It's all an unhappy blur, until I come to the night during the summer I was six that changed everything for me.

Around 2:00 a.m., I awoke to the sound of screaming outside my bedroom window. The screaming didn't seem to be coming from a person. I had never heard anything like it before. I woke my parents and we went out to the yard to investigate. There we found a baby rabbit, quivering and unable to move after a near-death encounter with some larger animal. Frozen in terror, she was incapable of fleeing, and allowed me to pick her up. Her mother was nowhere in sight, so I decided I had better bring her inside where she would be safe. I lay down on the

3

orange shag carpeting in the kitchen and placed her on my chest, where she could feel my heartbeat. Gradually she calmed down, giving only an occasional whimper.

That was the first time I can remember feeling love. Great waves of it seemed to be swirling around us, engulfing both my newfound friend and me. Though I could not have explained it in words, I knew on some level that this rabbit and I shared the same life, the same spirit, that we were connected to each other by something greater than the both of us, and something much bigger was running the show. A feeling of profound peace settled over me. Whenever I hear the phrase, "the peace that passeth understanding," it is that moment that comes to my mind. Though I had intended to stay awake all night, I drifted off to sleep. When I awoke later that morning, the rabbit's little face, just inches from my own, was the first thing I saw. She was still resting on my chest.

I think of that night as the first time an animal rescued me. I had been so tenuously attached to the world that a strong wind might have blown me away, but then I felt as if I belonged here. The mingling of the rabbit's tremulous little heartbeat with mine made my own heart feel big and strong and sufficient. In stroking her warm, silky fur, I discovered what my hands were for. To save an animal's life made sense of my own life.

As a passionate animal advocate with a degree in veterinary medicine, my life's work has been coming to the aid of other creatures and saving their lives when I can. What I discovered at six has continued to be true: in rescuing an animal, I rescue myself. This reciprocity between animals and humans is woven into the very fabric of creation. It is the ecology of Paradise.

NAMING THE ANIMALS

Newscasts usually conclude with what they call a human-interest story. It's like a dessert—a little something sweet to look forward to after dutifully consuming the day's accounts of war, crime, scandal, political infighting, health scares, and economic woes. Animal stories work best at getting viewers to hang in until the end. We learn of the latest clever and useful things that dogs are being trained to do, of pets being rescued from various perils or reunited with their families after being lost for years, and of wild animals who have adopted orphans from other species. Cute, funny, or moving stories of animals are perhaps the most universal of human interests. They make us feel good.

It's odd that a source of happiness at once so reliable and so universal isn't regarded as more significant. Why is it that we dwell on the parts of a newscast that make us anxious and depressed while dismissing our favorite part as mere fluff? Why isn't the segment that awakens our hearts and makes us smile the most important part?

I believe that the happiness we feel in relation to animals is immensely significant. I believe it is absolutely central to our physical, psychological, and spiritual well-being. The fleeting yet undeniable delight that we feel when we hear an animal story is the key to the riddle that has been stumping human philosophers for millennia: how did we lose our place in Paradise, and how do we get it back?

As the Quran tells the story, God assembled all of the angels and introduced them to Adam, telling them that he was putting Adam in charge of the paradise he had just created on Earth. The angels thought this was a really bad idea. Why turn Eden over to someone who was just going to create bloodshed and disorder, instead of to the angels who lived only to praise God?

So God assembled all the creatures of the Earth and said to the angels, "Tell me their names." The angels felt that this was an unfair question.

"How can we know what you haven't told us?" they protested.

Then God turned to Adam and asked him the names of the creatures. Adam was able to name every single one. Seeing Adam ace the test that they themselves had flunked, the angels figured God must know what he was doing after all.

In order to name something, we need to have perceived it clearly. It becomes personal—naming gives recognition to another living being. We are then more clearly able to tell the difference between one living being and other living beings. The more names we know, the more differentiated our perception is. If you've been paying close attention to dogs, you know a lot of breed names. If you pay even closer attention, you can tell the difference between individual dogs of the same breed and can call a dog by his or her personal name. In the United States, we have become much more personal with our companion animals. Years ago, people used to give their dogs names like Fido and they lived outside in doghouses. Now we give our dog companions the same names we give our children (and they sleep in our beds). The food-animal industry knows how powerful naming is. Pigs are called "units." How else could they bear to force living beings capable of emotions and feeling pain to exist in such horrific conditions? Not allowing these animals to have names makes it easier for the humans who work in this industry to betray the voices in their hearts, anesthetizing their compassion.

According to the Quran, God, the Source of all, highly prized the ability to give an animal a name. It was so important to him it became the sole factor he considered when deciding who should be his representative on Earth. Never mind that Adam was disorderly, prone to violence, and kept forgetting to pray. His coming up with a name for every single creature pleased God better than prayer.

You would think that, having won approval solely on this basis, humans would continue to give it the highest priority. You would expect everyone to spend an immense amount of time reciting litanies of animal names. You would expect us to venerate as saints and gurus those fellow humans who could tell sparrows apart well enough to address each flock member by a name of his or her own. It's odd that we don't.

The tales of Adam that appear in the Quran and the Bible were never meant as literal accounts of how the material world came to be. A creation myth is a story about the origin of a psychospiritual condition. On that level, the story of Adam tells us something best taken more literally than we usually would. Human history has carried us further and further away from a state we dimly recall as much happier. The primary symptom of that movement away from Paradise has been a growing estrangement from our fellow creatures. The fewer plants and animals we are able to recognize as individuals—recognize well enough to name—the more alienated we have come to feel from ourselves, the Earth and God, the Source.

Nearly every religion in the world tells some variation on the creation story: that living on Earth used to feel like living in Paradise. Yet the relevance of that point continues to escape us. We can't seem to wrap our minds around the fact that Paradise is *here*. Nor can we see the central importance of our fellow creatures to the meaning and purpose of human existence. The more sophisticated our theologies and philosophies and therapies become, the less they seem to have to say about animals. It is possible to become a doctor of philosophy without ever, in the course of one's scholarly reading, encountering a single animal's name. In our pursuit of an ever more elusive paradise, we do anything and everything except the one thing our Source specifically asked us to do.

ANCIENT FACTS AND MODERN SUPERSTITIONS

When children draw pictures of animals, they give the animals human-like facial expressions. This is true of children the world over. It is also true of the entertainment adults devise for children. In cartoons and storybooks, the animals talk, feel emotions, and solve problems. They have faults, virtues, personality quirks, and individual names. Animals in children's literature always have a soul life because children perceive animals as having souls.

The belief that every living thing has an individual soul is called *animism*. (*Anima*, which means "soul," is also the root of the word "animal.") Anthropologists have found this belief to be universal in children, though the children themselves don't think of it as a belief. It is, to them, one of the most obvious features of the world around them, and the most obvious way of interpreting what goes on in that world.

Animism is also the norm among adults in preindustrial cultures. As a general rule, the less technologically sophisticated a culture is, the more likely its adults are to view the world in an animistic way. The most obvious examples of this are indigenous tribal cultures whose religions incorporate spirit animals. But it is also true of many rural people who practice religions that are not officially animistic. In the paintings and tapestries of medieval Europe, the animals often look like children drew them. They have expressive, cartoonlike faces. These pictures come from a time when people had intimate daily contact with animals, and depended on their help with farming and hunting. On cold nights, they would bring their animals inside their homes and sleep alongside them for warmth—not just dogs and cats, but cows, oxen, horses, and sheep. Just as you know full well that your dog or cat (if you are fortunate enough to have one) has a soul, rural people can perceive the souls in the other animals with whom they have daily contact. If their religion teaches otherwise, they simply assume that, on this point, their religion doesn't know what it's talking about.

In avowedly animistic religions, animals are regarded as spirit guides, and gods are often depicted as animals. Such religions are more common in tribes than in nations, and when, as usually happens, a tribal culture gets conquered or absorbed by a nation, its religion gets conquered as well. Like nations themselves, the religions of nations tend to have a more centralized and hierarchical power structure. This is particularly true of the monotheistic religions, which consolidate all of the local deities into one God, and regard the veneration of animals as a heathen superstition.

Perhaps the misguided belief within modern, postindustrial religions that animals are lesser beings, simply neural networks firing, incapable of feelings or emotions, is the real "superstition." This belief can be called a modern superstition because it is not based on the experiences of contemporary people who know or live with animals. Believing that in place of thoughts, emotions, and aspirations, animals have only instincts and drives, that their lives are about nothing more than a Darwinian struggle for survival, could only take hold among people who don't know any animals personally. Like the dragons of medieval times, the soulless, instinct-driven animals imagined by postindustrial people are mythological beasts.

This modern belief is partly the result of ignorance (in this case, due to insufficient contact with animals), but for it to take hold, it also has to serve some psychological purpose. People have to be motivated to believe it, and motivated to convince others of it. So what is the motive for this particular false belief? Why does it appeal most to people who have attained a high level of prosperity and technological sophistication?

For an answer to that one, you need look no further than your last serving of chicken. As you probably know, most chickens nowadays come from factories rather than farms. These factory-raised chickens reach physical maturity four times faster than normal chickens. Their breasts are so big in proportion to their legs that they couldn't walk even if there were anywhere to walk *to*. There isn't, because they are packed together as tightly as passengers on a plane. Imagine being born on a fully booked flight, spending your entire life confined to your seat, and dying there. That's the life of the chicken whose flesh and eggs have become commodities. We would think it unpardonably cruel to do that to someone if we believed him capable of mental or emotional suffering.

Although I recommend a diet that does not include meat, that we eat chickens and their eggs is not the issue here. People in animist cultures are seldom vegetarian, and they often depend heavily on animal labor. The difference is that they don't regard animals as commodities. They understand and respect animals and assert that they have a willingness to serve—with their labor, with their companionship, with their milk and eggs and wool, and even with the surrender of their lives so that others may be nourished. Later in the book, I describe a deeper understanding of the prey-predator relationship, which is little understood by humans, especially in Western culture. It is this altruistic impulse in the animal's soul that we violate when, out of a sense of entitlement, we seize and exploit rather than permit the animal to give.

In the deepest sense, to name the animals is to recognize their dignity, their individuality, their nobility, and the meaning of their lives. Of late, we've really been falling down on the job.

WHAT WE DO TO ANIMALS WE DO TO OURSELVES

Prior to the Industrial Revolution, *humane* and *human* were just two different spellings of the same word. To be humane in the Humane

Society—sense meant the same thing as being human. It's probably no accident that we began to need a separate word to describe the compassionate treatment of animals around the time we invented the sweatshop. We started confining people to factories and treating them like commodities before we got the idea of doing it to chickens. We denied the dignity of the human laborer before we denied the dignity of the plough horse. We began thinking of "pets" as consumer goods only after we had come to conceive of ourselves and our fellow humans as mere consumers. Nowadays we have to add an "e" to connote what the word "human" is supposed to mean: someone who demonstrates that he or she has a soul by treating other souls with respect and consideration.

The word "humane" conveys a sense of honorable conduct: the obligation of the strong to care for the weak or, as Buddhists teach, the duty of higher beings toward lower beings. I'm all for honorable conduct if it gets the job done, but I believe that, in the final analysis, it doesn't. To be humane sounds like more of a nicety than a necessity. The chainsaws and bulldozers of necessity make short work of a nicety like saving the spotted owl. Insofar as the fate of animals depends on our adding an "e" to human, they will continue to be victimized.

Mahatma Gandhi said that "the greatness of a nation can be judged by the way its animals are treated." This is what makes respect for animals not just a nicety but a necessity. A society in which animals are oppressed and exploited, their dignity denied and their lives deprived of meaning, is as miserable for its human citizens as it is for the animals. Why? Because what we do to animals, we do to ourselves. When we eat the flesh of an animal who has been pumped full of antibiotics and hormones and subjected to constant stress, all of those toxins become part of our own bodies. When we destroy animal habitat, we destroy our own habitat as well. When our treatment of other living beings is dominated by economic expediency, humans, too, are cruelly treated. When we can no longer see the hurt in a neglected animal's eyes, we have become hard-hearted toward our own pain.

On a spiritual level, the belief in animal inferiority has infected humans themselves with an inferiority complex. We can't look down on animals without also looking down on those aspects of our nature that we have in common with them. The spiritual pecking order that places us above the animals places us below the angels, so we tend to conceive of spiritual betterment as becoming more angel-like. Hierarchical spirituality values objectivity over feeling, abstraction over sensation, achievement over pleasure, the universal over the personal, the mind over the body. It encourages top growth at the expense of root growth. Unable to reach deep into the earth, where our nourishment lies, we become parched and desiccated. We also become incurably lonely— alienated not just from the Earth and from our fellow creatures, but from the parts of our own being that lie south of the neck.

Because hierarchical spirituality places God, the Source, at the very top of the pecking order, for many believers "God" seems unreachably remote. Whether we conceive of God as literally living in Heaven or not, he (or she) might as well be there for all the hope we have of direct contact. The belief that our Source is somewhere "up there" leads to the belief that we have to get "up there" to connect. Many people conceive of this happening in the afterlife. The Earth is just a place of temporary exile where one proves one's worthiness to go to the place where the Source of all exists. If we regard the Earth as just a transient residence, it's hardly any wonder that we turn it into a slum.

The hierarchical view that holds humans inferior to angels and animals inferior to humans is based on a faulty premise. All of God's (or whatever name you choose) creations are perfect, and it is impossible for one perfect thing to be inferior to another perfect thing. All the creatures of the Earth have lives of meaning and purpose, aside from the values we place on them. Now more than ever, the nonhuman beings that share the Earth with us have been entrusted to our care. How we value all life forms and how we treat them are true measures of our humanity.

THE RECIPROCITY OF PARADISE

For much of my life, I found it easier to relate to animals than to people. Animals seemed friendlier, and they didn't judge me. It didn't matter that I wasn't much good at saying things in words because animals seemed to understand all that I left unspoken. Yet these days I am finding that it is animals who propel me into fuller engagement with the human world. I so urgently want to advocate for animals that I am able to overcome my dread of standing on a stage and speaking into a microphone. The animals have given me the courage to do what I need to do on their behalf, and they have helped me to find my voice. The little girl who could barely rub two words together is now writing a book.

The grim truth that what we do to animals we do to ourselves has a joyful corollary: what we do *for* animals, we do for ourselves. If you have a dog, you've already experienced this principle at work. When you walk your dog to give him exercise, you get exercise too. When you pet or play with a dog, he enjoys a release of a feel-good hormone called oxytocin, and the level of stress hormones in his bloodstream declines. While you are petting a dog, the exact same thing happens in your own body. Medical researchers have discovered that people who live with companion animals recover faster and more fully from serious illnesses. For the elderly, having an animal friend improves mental alertness and diminishes feelings of social isolation. Animals have also been shown to be of enormous benefit to people suffering from psychological conditions or emotional traumas that make it difficult for them to connect with their fellow humans. When given an animal to care for, soldiers afflicted with PTSD experience fewer anxiety attacks. Incarcerated felons begin to feel like they're worth something, often for the first time in their lives.

This reciprocity between human and animal well-being is equally present on a spiritual level. What all creation myths have in common is the idea that whatever catastrophic event put an end to Paradise applied only to humans. Wild animals continued to experience the Earth as the best of all possible worlds. They were fundamentally happy and continue to be fundamentally happy to this day. They can be—and deeply wish to be—a source of happiness for human beings. We cannot find our way back to Paradise without them.

If we look at the external lives of animals, we may have trouble seeing what there is to be happy about. The things that worry and scare us happen to animals too. They live at the mercy of the elements, and they don't always find enough to eat. They grow old and they die—sometimes in ways that appear terrifying to us. Their young often perish before they reach adulthood. What seems even worse, from a human point of view, is that the harsh material facts of animal existence appear to be the whole story. They are not offset by the projects and achievements that give meaning to human lives, nor by the various entertainments we devise to distract ourselves. If animals are indeed happy under conditions that we would find intolerable, their inner lives must be very different from ours. And indeed, that is the case.

For animals, the Source is not "up there"—it is a universal connection, like one mind, which embodies what they are made of and what everything else is made of. They breathe, eat, and swim in the Source. When the sun comes out, they feel the warmth of the Source, and when the rains come, they feel the wetness of the Source; the wind is the Source of all, blowing over their feathers or fur. The same is true when they are injured, or when they suffer a loss and feel grief. Because God, the Source, is equally in all pleasurable things and all difficult things, nothing could ever occur that would separate them from the Source. They cannot even conceive of such a separation. Their inability to conceive of it is what makes life on Earth fundamentally happy for them, even when it is hard.

We humans can fleetingly imagine feeling this way. We, too, may feel the presence of our Source in the natural world when nature is on its good behavior: expressing itself in a gorgeous sunset or a towering redwood or the song of a robin. What trips us up are the painful parts. We think pain ought to be prevented. *Someone* is supposed to be preventing it.

I believe we have this idea that bad things ought to be prevented from happening. Every species on Earth expresses a unique aspect of the divine mind. What we humans embody is the part of the divine mind that sees room for improvement in creation, the part that cannot be completely at peace with seeing any creature suffer. We not only think that pain ought to be prevented, but also try to figure out *how* to prevent it. And it must be said that we're often quite ingenious in this regard. Our unique combination of solicitude and ingenuity just might be why all the other creatures are now in our care.

Because we think about the future more than animals do, we are better than they are at foreseeing consequences. So it is ironic that when animal species become endangered, it is almost always the unforeseen result of human activity. We have forgotten to take our impact on the animals into account, or we haven't considered it a priority. But human foresight is also really good at recognizing such trends before it is too late and figuring out how to reverse them. Animals depend on us for this, because problems caused by humans are usually too complicated and unfamiliar for the animals to solve on their own.

When the whooping crane population dwindled to just fourteen breeding pairs, illegal hunting by humans was largely to blame. Yet it is human ingenuity that is now saving the whooping crane from extinction. Conservation workers captured the few remaining birds and moved them to a more protected location. While this enabled the cranes to increase their numbers, it also disrupted their migratory patterns: the cranes didn't know the route from their new home. It was up to their human rescuers to teach them. Since young birds "imprint" on the first creature they see after hatching, believing that creature to be their mother, the humans dressed up in crane costumes so that the hatchlings would imprint on them. When it was time to migrate, the same people got into light planes and took off in the direction of the old migratory route, hoping the flock would follow. It worked.

The very quality that makes us helpful to other creatures—our ability to see room for improvement in the world—makes us less happy than they are. Sometimes it makes us downright miserable. Because we're better than animals at foreseeing problems, we're also prone to worrying. We imagine problems that don't exist, and then create new problems in our efforts to solve the nonexistent ones. We're so busy worrying and trying to improve the world that we find it almost impossible to just relax and enjoy the present moment. Unlike all other living beings, we have a lot of trouble accepting death. Though we see that it is inevitable, we can't help regarding it as a mistake. We alternate between brooding about it, trying to prevent it, and trying to ignore it. We also have trouble accepting ourselves. We see so much room for improvement in ourselves that we have a hard time believing that we are lovable.

This is why the need between animals and humans is mutual. They need us to protect them and we need them to help us to feel happier.

We can't make ourselves happier by directly emulating animals, because our nature is different from theirs in some fundamental ways. But when we love animals and form close bonds with them, some of their happiness rubs off on us. To watch them enjoying their lives makes us smile. Their good moods are infectious. Their affection for us has the power to reach the place in us that feels unworthy of being loved, and in feeling how they love us, we can feel how God loves us too.

If we are open to it, an even deeper rapport becomes possible. We can come to share their thoughts, feelings, and perceptions, to look at the world through their eyes and see what they find so good about it. In this way, animals can become our spiritual teachers. Animals have taught me to perceive the connectedness of all living things and to experience for myself the joy they experience in this connectedness. They have taught me to accept the limits of my own understanding and to relax into the mystery of existence. They have taught me how to be less afraid of death, and less afraid of all the other things that are not under my control. They have taught me how to lighten up and enjoy the present moment. Most of all, they have taught me how to find repose in the certainty that I am loved.

You might be wondering how this is possible. Animals can't talk, so how can we know what they're thinking and feeling? When I say that animals experience everything in the world as a part of God, the Source, how in the world do I know that? When shamans say that animals give their lives willingly so that others may eat, how do they know?

Animals are able to communicate telepathically. People have this ability too. In fact, it is often animals who awaken it in us. Intuitive exchanges between people and animals were the norm throughout most of our time on the planet. (They are still the norm in the few animistic cultures that remain on Earth.) What we now call extrasensory perception (ESP) used to be an everyday occurrence. People took it entirely for granted that you didn't need to exchange words in order to communicate thoughts and feelings. It stopped being the norm because we talked ourselves out of it around the same time we talked ourselves out of believing that animals had souls. The inability to recognize a soul when we see one is what causes our inborn telepathic powers to go on the blink. If we persist in ignoring our intuition long enough, it eventually atrophies to the point where it is no longer discernable. But this is easily remedied. When we start to pay attention again, our telepathic ability comes back, good as new.

You don't have to take my word for it. Scientific research has demonstrated what I am saying to the satisfaction of all but the most hardened skeptics. In the next chapter I will present the scientific evidence. In a later chapter, I will teach you step by step how to reengage with universal reality, the universal mind, where all creation is inseparable—the reality in which animals exist. In that reality, we are able to hear the silent universal language of animals and engage in inner conversations with them. You don't need to believe in advance that it is possible, for you will be able to judge this from your own experience.

GETTING ADAM BACK ON TASK

For most of recorded history, humans have related to just a small number of the millions of species on Earth. The other species lived in wilderness areas where the human population was sparse or nonexistent and got along very well without us. It is only in the past couple of centuries that humans have begun to encroach on their habitats, and that encroachment has grown exponentially in our own lifetimes. This is both because the human population has exploded, and because we are living in a style that makes intensive and unprecedented demands on the Earth's resources. The safety most species found in their isolation from us is rapidly vanishing.

This drastic change in the physical ecosystem has led to a corresponding change in the spiritual ecosystem. Wild animals have discovered that they cannot go on living in blissful ignorance of human activities and human concerns. They are feeling a new need to understand what we are about, and to communicate to us what they are about. Their survival depends on coming into a new kind of relationship with us. Consequently, I have written this book, which has been gestating my whole life. It is also why teaching the wisdom I have learned over the course of my life, from interactions with both wildlife and companion animals, consumes most of my time now.

A few years ago, I spent several glorious weeks in the Timbavati region of South Africa, visiting the sacred land of the white lions, and Kruger Park, where the largest land mammals on Earth still roam in freedom. On my last day at the park, as I was being driven away in a jeep, very sad to be leaving, a large herd of buffalo suddenly emerged from the bush and stepped onto the road. Our driver halted, waiting for them to cross. But instead of moving on, the buffalo stopped in the middle of the road and turned to stare at us. It was as if they were one mind, every body motionless, every head pointed in the same direction, staring at us with startling intensity. My eyes darted around the herd, looking for exceptions. These animals were used to seeing people and I found it hard to imagine that they could really be as interested as they appeared. But there were no exceptions. Every single member of the herd, even the very young, was standing stock-still, gazing at us with an air of solemn formality. In that moment, I understood that their sudden appearance had been intentional, that they were a sort of delegation, and that I was the one they had come to see. Their message, delivered telepathically with one voice, reverberated in my mind and heart. It was: *"Do not forget us. Do not forget us. Teach others in your land what you know; do not forget us."*

One reason for their appeal was obvious: they and other animals are endangered and urgently need us to address their plight. But something less obvious came through to me as well. The animals feel that this urgency is *mutual*. Their own suffering has made them aware of human suffering. More frequent contact with us has sensitized them to what troubles us. They feel our anxiety and our confusion and, most of all, our loneliness. The pain of being disconnected from the Earth, from each other, from our fellow creatures, and from the Source of all life is the worst pain they can imagine, and they are concerned about us. They understand even better than we do that the suffering we inflict on them is an expression of our own suffering, and that their physical situation cannot get better unless the human spiritual condition gets better. They want to help. It is for that reason that they are making a concerted effort to connect with us telepathically. They have asked me to teach my fellow humans how to hear them.

So I teach what I have learned over the course of my life from animals—beginning as a young child connecting through the heart, soul to soul, then through my vet work with companion animals and wildlife, and as an animal advocate around the world. The sacred connection between humans and animals has been the theme of my life.

Often since my encounter with the buffalo in South Africa I have been haunted, almost obsessed with the message they sent on that day: *"Do not forget us."* Yet when I become overagitated in my sense of urgency about it, I sometimes hear a more soft-spoken voice coming from the same delegation, speaking out of a deep and patient love. It says, *"And we do not forget you."*

Chapter 2

How Can We Know
What Animals Are
Thinking and Feeling?

Intuition is all that matters.

—Albert Einstein

There are more things in this world than you have ever dreamed of.

—William Shakespeare

Dave Gaillard was cross-country skiing near Yellowstone National Park when an avalanche struck. The family dog, a Welsh Corgi named Oly, had accompanied him on the outing. Rescuers assumed that the dog had been killed along with Gaillard. But four days later, Oly was found sitting outside the family's motel room, staring at the door. Somehow he had survived, and found his way back to the motel over a distance of four miles.

That story, which was reported by the AP wire service in January of 2012, is the most recent addition to a large body of heroic animal-return tales. The most famous of these are jaw-dropping in their sheer improbability. There is the case of Minosch, a German cat who became separated from her family while on vacation and traveled 1,500 miles to return home, and Bobby, a collie lost in Indiana who turned

up at his family's new home in Oregon, having somehow traversed the
Rocky Mountains and hiked a distance of 3,000 miles. Most astonishing of all is the tale of Prince, a dog living in London during World
War I. After the man of the house was sent to fight in France, Prince
became depressed and refused to eat, then disappeared. The soldier's
wife searched for several weeks before reluctantly breaking the news to
her husband in a letter. By return post, her husband informed her that
Prince was with him! Somehow the dog had managed to make his way
from London to the coast, secure passage across the English Channel,
and find his master among a half million other soldiers on a battlefield
riddled with exploding shells.

Stories like these confirm what many of us would like to believe
about our companion animals: if separated they might undertake peril-
ous journeys to be reunited with us, and that they are smart enough to
find their way over vast distances, and by routes that they have never
been taught. The animal's intelligence and his love for his human companion are inseparable in our minds, as if devotion itself served as some
sort of GPS device. Yet it is precisely because these stories are so deeply
gratifying to us on an emotional level that our intellects regard them
skeptically. We are inclined to believe that the more wish-fulfilling the
tale, the more likely it is to be legend or a hoax.

Scientists who have studied the phenomenon are at a loss to explain
how animals find their way back to their people, but they have demonstrated through controlled experiments that some animals do indeed
possess this ability. The zoologist F. H. Herrick conducted the earliest
of these experiments during the first decade of the twentieth century.
One day he brought his cat to work with him at Western Reserve University in Cleveland. When they arrived at his office, the cat escaped.
That evening, when Herrick returned to his home, he discovered that
the cat had returned there as well. Since he had carried the cat to work
in a bag and traveled by streetcar, the cat could not have observed the
route or followed a scent trail. Puzzled, Herrick went on to test the cat
by carrying it in a bag to various locations within a three-mile radius of
his house. The cat always found its way back.

In the early 1930s, the naturalist Bastian Schmidt undertook a similar series of experiments on sheepdogs. He would drive dogs in a closed van by a roundabout route to various locations that they had never been before, then release them. Trained observers followed the dog from a distance. The dogs consistently returned home, usually by the most direct route, rather than by the route that they had been driven. The observers noted that the dogs walked steadily and purposefully, as if they knew where they were going. They were not sniffing in search of a trail. Nor can they have been relying on visual clues, since they had been unable to see anything on their journey to the release point.

Rupert Sheldrake, a Cambridge naturalist and biochemist, replicated these experiments for a BBC documentary filmed in 1996. His subject was a border collie-terrier mix named Pepsi, who belonged to a Leicester resident named Clive Rudkin. Over the years, Pepsi had gotten loose on fourteen separate occasions and each time had managed to reunite with Clive within a few hours. On many of these occasions, she returned not to Clive's house, but to the home of one of his friends or relatives. In all, she managed to find her way to six different destinations that she had, at one time or another, visited with Clive. For the filmed experiment, Sheldrake attached a GPS device to Pepsi so that her movements could be tracked. He and Clive drove her by taxi to a street corner two miles from Clive's house, keeping her on the taxi floor so that she could not observe the route. Four hours after being released, she had not, as expected, returned to the house. Instead, she was found lying in the garden of Clive's sister, which was located about a mile from the release point. The GPS records indicated that Pepsi had immediately headed north—the opposite of the direction in which she had seen the taxi departing. Instead of attempting to retrace the route home, Pepsi had set off for the nearest familiar location, arriving there by a route she had never traveled before.

Like people, animals often navigate within their ranges—the areas that they habitually frequent—using their physical senses, orienting themselves through familiar sights, sounds, and scents. But many animals have, in addition, the ability to orient to a destination itself, finding their way to it by the most direct route, even if it is a route they have never traveled before, and from a departure point with which they have no previous familiarity. It is as if they are following an attraction, be-ing magnetized by the destination itself. This ability, called "homing" has been confirmed in migrating birds and in some wild animals, such as wolves, who navigate ranges that may extend for hundreds of miles.

What is particularly striking in the case of companion animals is that the destination may be a person rather than a place. Oly, Bobby, and Prince found their way back to beloved humans who were many miles from their usual residences. Pepsi had a knack not just for finding Clive, but for finding Clive's friends and relations. Joseph B. Rhine, the parapsychological researcher who coined the term ESP, called this phe-nomenon *psi-trailing*. In 1962, he and his associate, Sara Feather, pub-lished a study in which they investigated fifty-four reported cases of it. Of these, they eliminated cases in which the returning animal could not be conclusively identified as the one who had been lost (as opposed to a look-alike stray). To rule out the possibility that the animal had been simply wandering around at random in search of home, they elimi-nated all the cases in which the distance traveled was less than thirty miles. The cases that meet these strict criteria are pretty astonishing.

In one of them, a boy had befriended a racing pigeon who bore the number 167 on his leg ring. Later the boy fell ill and was airlifted to a hospital 105 miles away. One night the boy noticed a pigeon fluttering outside the window of his hospital room. At his request, a nurse opened the window and, when the pigeon came in, examined its leg band. As the boy had predicted, the number on the band was 167. Though the ability of pigeons to home over great distances is well known, it does not explain how the pigeon knew the boy was hospitalized and found its way to that particular hospital.

Another report deemed reliable because there were so many wit-nesses to it was the case of Hector, the terrier companion of a ship's captain named Willem Mante. While on shore leave in Vancouver, Hector had broken loose and gone off to explore the town. He had done the same thing on previous shore leaves, always returning to the ship before it was time to set sail. But this time he did not show up, and a de-spondent Mante was obliged to depart for Japan without him. The fol-lowing morning, a crew member on another ship docked in Vancouver harbor saw a terrier board the vessel, sniff around for a few minutes, then disembark. Three other crews observed the dog doing the same thing on their ships. Later the dog was discovered stowing away on a ship that had already left port, bound for Japan. When the ship docked in Tokyo, nineteen days later, the dog leapt into the water and swam excitedly toward a small nearby craft that was manned by members of Mante's crew. After exploring and rejecting at least four other ships, Hector had somehow managed to choose the one that would reunite him with his friend.

The journey of Bobby, the collie lost in Indiana who turned up at his family's new home in Oregon, was pieced together after the fact by a writer named Charles Alexander. He placed advertisements in newspapers along Bobby's most likely route, asking for information from anyone who might have encountered the dog. The accounts he received in reply were quite consistent in their description of Bobby's behavior. A number of humans had attempted to befriend him. He would accept such hospitality only briefly before escaping to continue his westward journey. On one occasion, he had leapt into an icy and turbulent river to avoid capture. He had also managed to escape from a van that was headed eastward. When Alexander plotted the locations and dates of Bobby's various appearances on a map, they demonstrated that the dog had traveled steadily in the right direction for the entire three months that he had been lost.

Rhine regarded incidents such as these as evidence that some animals, like some humans, have ESP. Of course, the cases we have described here are exceptional. Thousands of cats and dogs are lost every year and unable to find their way home by psi-trailing. But there are other forms of ESP in animals that occur so frequently that they can almost be considered the norm.

HAPPY ANTICIPATION IN DOGS AND CATS

The rule in my house is that dogs are not allowed on the white sofa in the living room. Pepper, who has been in our family for nearly fifteen years, is well aware of this rule. He is also aware that I am the only one who enforces it. My son and daughter don't care if Pepper sits on the white sofa, and often they find him lounging there when they return home unexpectedly. I myself have never caught him in the act. According to my kids, Pepper gets up from the sofa and moves to his own bed fifteen to twenty minutes before I arrive home. He has been doing this for years, and he never gets it wrong, even though my comings and goings are unpredictable and my kids themselves don't know when to expect me.

It turns out that many dogs have the ability to know when a human who is important to them is on the way home. Rupert Sheldrake, who is well known for his research into the psychic abilities of both animals and humans, has made an extensive study of the phenomenon. Over the years, he had received hundreds of reports of dogs who would appear excited and station themselves by a door or window shortly before their human guardians arrived home. When he surveyed friends, colleagues, and audience members at his lectures, nearly two-thirds of them reported that their dogs did this. To find out whether this was typical of the population as a whole, Sheldrake conducted a survey. Households in several different American and British towns were telephoned at random. Those who had dogs were asked, "Have you or has anyone in your household ever noticed your animal getting agitated before a family member arrives home?" More than half of those surveyed responded in the affirmative. Sheldrake believes that the actual number of dogs displaying anticipatory behavior is probably higher, since respondents who lived alone had no way of knowing what their dogs were doing while they were away.

In and of itself, anticipatory behavior is not proof of ESP. Routine is the more obvious explanation: a dog can predict a person's arrival because it occurs at approximately the same time every day. Assuming this to be the case, many people find their dog's anticipatory behavior unremarkable until they break their routine—for instance, coming home much earlier than expected—and find that it has nevertheless occurred. Some people even experiment with their dogs, varying their routine on purpose to see what will happen. Over the years, Sheldrake received over a thousand reports from people whose dogs were able to anticipate unpredictable returns.

Once routine is eliminated, the next most likely explanation is that the dogs are picking up on sensory cues. They can smell the approaching human, or they are responding to a familiar sound, such as footsteps on the sidewalk, or a car pulling in to the driveway. The behavior of other household members might also tip them off: for example, a husband who starts cooking dinner shortly before his wife comes home from work. Before a person or animal can be said to be exercising ESP, all such cues need to be eliminated. This is what Sheldrake went on to do in a series of experiments.

At his request, twenty people kept logs of their dog's anticipatory behavior. They noted where the person went and how long he or she was away, the method of travel, and whether or not the person had arrived home at the expected time. They also noted failures and false alarms. One of the most detailed and impressive logs concerned a terrier named Jaytee and his guardian, Pamela Smart. Jaytee was unusual in that he would begin waiting by the window a half hour before Pamela's returns, rather than the ten minutes or so that is more typical of dogs. This made it unlikely that his anticipation was being triggered by a scent or a sound. When she began the log, Pamela was working as a secretary and came home at approximately the same time every day. Her family assumed that Jaytee had figured out her routine. But after she was laid off from her job when she was looking for work, her comings and goings became unpredictable. Her parents often had no idea when she would return until they saw Jaytee go to the window. According to the log, Jaytee was getting it right nine times out of ten.

When he analyzed the log, Sheldrake discovered that the length of time Jaytee spent waiting by the window varied from one absence to the next, and corresponded to the length of time Pamela was spending in transit. Apparently Jaytee began anticipating her arrival at the moment she set off for home. To test this hypothesis, Sheldrake set up a video camera to record Jaytee's behavior while another camera followed Pamela. At a randomly selected time, she was given a message to return home by taxi. Eleven seconds after she received this message, Jaytee went to the window and remained there for the duration of her journey. The experiment was repeated, varying the duration of Pamela's absence, the length of her return journey, and her mode of transport. Jaytee anticipated her accurately regardless of whether she traveled on foot, by bicycle, by train, by taxi, or in her own car, and sometimes began his vigil when she was nearly an hour away. It is therefore extremely unlikely that he could have been responding to any sensory clues. The anticipatory behavior began whenever her homeward journey began, suggesting that Jaytee was somehow picking up on Pamela's *intention* to return.

This hypothesis was further supported by some of the "false alarms" reported in other logs. People would often note that when their dog mistakenly anticipated a return, they had in fact set off for home at that time, and then either changed their mind or encountered some delay. Sheldrake repeated the Jaytee experiment with another dog, a Rhodesian ridgeback named Kane, and his human friend Sarah. Like Jaytee, Kane showed anticipatory behavior in nine trials out of ten, and the duration of this behavior correlated with the duration of Sarah's return journey.

The phenomenon is so widespread that Sheldrake felt compelled to explain why it doesn't occur with *all* dogs. As mentioned previously, some people may be unaware of the behavior because there is no one at home to observe the dog when they are out. Sheldrake also theorized that some dogs who possess the ability are not motivated to exercise it. For anticipatory behavior to occur, the dog needs to have reason to feel excited about the human's arrival. If the bond between the dog and the human is not strong, or if the homecoming human doesn't reward the dog with an immediate and affectionate greeting, the dog has no incentive to wait by a door or window. Finally, Sheldrake points out that with animals, just as with people, some individuals are more psychically sensitive than others.

A related form of anticipatory behavior is responding to a ringing telephone when a favorite human is on the line. This is particularly common in cats. The animal will show excitement and run toward the phone as soon as rings, and before it is answered—but only in response to a particular caller. Some cats even run to the phone just *before* it rings. After eliminating all the cases that might be explained by routine (that is, the person calling regularly and at predictable times) Sheldrake was left with seventeen reports of cats and eight reports of dogs who appear to possess telepathic "caller ID."

Humans, too, have this ability, apparently to an even greater extent than animals do. Along with David Jay Brown, Sheldrake conducted a random survey on the phenomenon in 2001. Their findings:

- 78 percent of the people surveyed said that they have had the experience of telephoning someone who said that they were just thinking about telephoning them.
- 47 percent of the respondents said that they had had the experience of knowing who was calling them when the phone rang without any possible cue.
- 68 percent of those surveyed said that they had thought about a person that they haven't seen for a while, who had then telephoned them that same day.

WARNINGS AND PREMONITIONS

In the hour before the 2004 tsunami struck, many people noticed that the animals were acting weird. Cicadas stopped rattling and birds stopped singing. Dogs refused to go outdoors. Elephants trumpeted in alarm and stampeded toward the hills. Relative to the human population, very few animals were drowned. They seemed to know what was coming, and what to do about it. But how?

Wildlife experts speculate that animals, who on the whole have a more acute sense of hearing than we do, might have heard the earthquake that triggered the tidal wave, or perhaps felt its vibrations. They might have noticed some subtle electromagnetic change in the air, or in the earth's magnetic field. If so, what remains unexplained is how the animals recognized the significance of these changes and knew that they needed to flee toward higher ground.

Animals also anticipate earthquakes—something seismologists admit that they themselves are unable to do. The bizarre behavior of animals in the days leading up to a major quake is so well known that in the 1970s Chinese seismologists began training people to watch for it. In mid-December of 1974 these observers noticed that snakes were coming out of hibernation and that rats had abandoned their burrows to congregate in the open, huddling together in large groups, many of them so disoriented that they were easily caught. By the beginning of February, domestic and farm animals were showing signs of panic. Based on these animal warnings, officials decided to evacuate the city of Haicheng on the morning of February 4. At 7:36 p.m. the same evening, an earthquake measuring 7.3 on the Richter scale struck, destroying half the buildings in the city. But for the timely evacuation, tens of thousands of people might have lost their lives.

During World War II, many Londoners noticed that their dogs seemed to know when an air raid was coming. Before the sirens sounded the official alarm, these dogs would howl or whimper or hide. Some of them even attempted to lead their families to the air-raid shelter. Cats and birds would also display signs of agitation. Sheldrake points out that it is unlikely that the animals were hearing the approaching bombers. On average, the animals began showing distress a half hour or more before a raid. Since the planes flew at a speed of 250 mph, the animals would have to have heard them when they were at least 125 miles away. Furthermore, dogs and cats are not normally upset by the sound of passing aircraft. Even if it was hearing that tipped them off, the animals were somehow able to distinguish between an innocent plane and one that was approaching with intent to harm.

Many people who live with animals have noticed that their cat or dog becomes solicitous of them when they are feeling unwell. A cat who is normally aloof may come sit in the sick person's lap; a normally rambunctious dog may tone himself down when his human friend isn't up to romping or running. In some cases, the ability of animals to sense illness in a human has been lifesaving.

Epileptics frequently discover that their canine companion can tell in advance when they are about to have a seizure—something epileptics themselves are not always able to detect in time to take appropriate action. In addition to knowing that a seizure is coming, these dogs seem to know what to do about it. They will attempt to lead the person to a safe place, or to pull her to the ground, sometimes lying on top of her to prevent injury. One woman reports that if her dog senses an impending seizure while she is in the bathtub, he will open the drain to prevent her from drowning. Dogs who live with diabetics display similar behavior, raising alarm when they sense that the diabetic's blood sugar has dropped to dangerously low levels. Val Strong, who trains service dogs, has observed that some dogs display only subtle signs of concern when a seizure is impending. When trained to be more demonstrative, they can become reliable protectors of their human companions, allowing their people to lead more normal lives.

Dogs are also able to detect cancer. In one case, a dog sniffed constantly at a mole and eventually tried to bite it off. The mole turned out to be a malignant melanoma that, thanks to the dog, was discovered and removed early enough to prevent the cancer from spreading. Another dog displayed a similar preoccupation with a small cyst on a woman's foot that doctors had dismissed as a harmless wart. As a result, she sought the second opinion that probably saved her life. Apparently dogs identify cancer by some telltale scent. By sniffing urine samples, dogs have been able to detect bladder cancer with 98 percent reliability, and they have a similar success rate at detecting lung and breast cancers by sniffing a sample of the patient's breath.

You might be noticing a common thread. In all of these examples, the possibility that animals are picking up on sensory clues cannot be completely eliminated. In the case of cancer, we know for certain that they are using their physical senses. The mystery is how the animals know the *meaning* of whatever it is that they perceive. How does the cancer-detecting dog know that what he smells is a threat to his human companion? How does the seizure-detecting dog know, without being trained, what she needs to do to protect an epileptic or a diabetic?

Human intuition is mysterious in the same way. Under laboratory conditions, parapsychological investigators are able to completely eliminate the possibility of sensory input. They define ESP as the ability to know something without any help whatsoever from the physical senses. But human intuition doesn't normally arise under laboratory conditions. Physical sensations—particularly sensations too subtle or fleeting to register in our conscious awareness—may play a part in it. For example, during ovulation, women produce a scent called a phero- mone. If you hold a sample of the stuff under a man's nose, he will say he can't smell anything, yet research has shown that when exposed to the pheromone, men feel an increased attraction to the opposite sex. Men, like animals, can tell when a female is "in heat." They might insist that they don't know, yet their behavior demonstrates that, on a sub- conscious level, they do know. There could be all sorts of sensory cues like this that never reach our conscious awareness.

People who are highly intuitive somehow pick up on subtle cues— whether sensory or extrasensory—and interpret them correctly, of- ten without having any idea how they're doing it. While it is true that physical senses are more acute in some animals than they are in hu- mans, this alone does not explain why animals are, on the whole, more psychically sensitive than we are. Animals seem to be better at paying attention to whatever it is that they are sensing, better at interpreting it, and better at trusting it. If we could get inside the minds of animals and understand how they are processing their experience, we would probably find that they have a lot to teach us about how to use our own intuition more effectively.

THE LIMITATIONS OF EXPERIMENT

On the evening of April 14, 1865, President Lincoln's dog went ber- serk. Though he normally accepted Lincoln's comings and goings with composure, that night he began howling, urgently and piteously, when the President and Mrs. Lincoln left the White House to attend a play. Nothing would calm the dog and no one could understand the reason for his extreme agitation. He was still howling when the report finally came that the President had been shot.

Over the years, Sheldrake collected 239 similar stories involving cats or dogs. In many of them, the animal inexplicably began shivering, whining, or howling at the exact moment when, it was later learned, a beloved and absent human was meeting with sudden death. This is a form of ESP that some animals and some humans have in common:

the ability to sense from a distance when a loved one is in danger or distress.

With this phenomenon, unlike psi-trailing or anticipatory behavior, researchers cannot so readily move from anecdotal evidence to controlled experiment, for to intentionally inflict distress on an animal in order to test its effect on that animal's intuition would be cruel. Emotional connectedness is a key factor in the prescience of animals (and of people too)—a factor that cannot be fully controlled in a scientific experiment even if one is so heartless as to attempt it.

Much as we crave the kind of certainty that experimental science provides, we have to recognize that not everything we wish to know is susceptible to absolute proof. When we distance ourselves from a living creature in order to study it objectively, the very thing we most want to know may hide itself from us. Rupert Sheldrake became sensitized to this difficulty early in his training as a biochemist. He writes, "It was an essential part of the biology curriculum to dissect nerves from the severed legs of frogs and stimulate them electrically to make the muscles twitch. For the study of enzymes in rat livers, we first had to decapitate the rats, their blood spurting down the laboratory sink. A love of animals had led me to study biology, and this is where it had taken me. Something had gone wrong."

Though they have yet to explain exactly how it works, scientists have proven the existence of ESP in both people and animals beyond all reasonable doubt. I began by presenting some of this evidence in order to lend scientific weight to what many animal lovers already know. Yet science is not *how* they know it. Animal lovers have insight into the minds of animals *because* they are animal lovers.

We humans reveal the deepest secrets of our inner lives only to those whom we trust because they love us. The same is true of animals. If you want to truly know them, you have to surrender some of your objectivity, allowing yourself to feel for them and with them. When you do this, you leave the realm of scientific certainty. You open yourself to the possibility of being mistaken, or of being considered a flake even if you are not mistaken. That is a risk I'm going to have to run, for what I want to talk about in this book is the spiritual life of animals.

We wouldn't expect science to tell us much about the inner life of a saint or mystic. Transcendent experiences cannot be quantified or explained or replicated under controlled conditions. This is as true of animal spirituality as it is of human spirituality. The difference is that humans can articulate their inner experience in words. They can't always express it well, but at the very least they can let us know when we are jumping to a mistaken conclusion. Intuitions into an animal's inner life are harder to confirm because they are harder to refute. If we are getting it wrong, how will an animal set us straight?

When people want to know what animals are thinking, our assumption tends to be that we need either to learn the animal's language or to teach the animal our own. Both endeavors are arduous and have, to date, yielded only modest results. Since, with the exception of a few birds in the parrot family, animals can't talk, we have to rely on observable behavior to confirm that we have understood them, or that they have understood us.

Andrea Turkalo of The Elephant Listening Project has been observing African elephants for two decades in the hope of compiling an elephant dictionary. Her method is to record elephant vocalizations and then watch to see what happens next. For example, if the herd takes evasive action after a particular call is sounded, the call is probably a warning. The handful of elephant "words" she has been able to decipher after twenty years of study is only a very small fraction of the elephant sounds she has recorded. Presumably all of these sounds have meanings, but human ears are not as attuned as elephant ears to the distinction between one sound and another, and if a sound is not accompanied by some behavior, its meaning remains a mystery. Scientists have encountered the same difficulty when studying other animals, such as dolphins, who have a large "vocabulary" of sounds that apparently mean something to others of their species. It is still unclear whether these sounds amount to what humans mean by language, since a sound can be communicative without being a word. (Consider, for example, a human moan or scream.) Recent research from the School of Biology, University of St Andrews, confirms what others have found regarding the distinctive "signature whistle" of every dolphin. The whistle serves as individual identification, like a name, so the individual can communicate to the rest of the pod, quickly and efficiently (sound travels four and a half to five times faster through water than through air, so although they have excellent eyesight, they use sound). Dolphins in distress sound out their whistles extremely loudly, causing the others to swim toward them. Like a human mother and child, a young calf and her mother stay united by calling to each other, also expressing emotional states. Pods of dolphins coordinate, strategize, and gather fish using vocalizations.

We believe that a dog has understood our words when he or she responds to commands like *come, sit,* and *stay.* Many dogs demonstrate that they also know the meaning of other words that particularly interest them, like *walk, drive,* and *vet.* One linguistically gifted dog, a border collie named Rico, became famous for his ability to identify dozens of his toys by name. But this understanding could only be conveyed by obedience to a fetch command. A word or phrase that evokes a consistent response might more accurately be termed a *stimulus* than the thing linguistics experts mean by *language.* In any event, a shared language in which rapport can only be confirmed by obedience is not very productive of interesting exchanges.

One of the great breakthroughs in animal communication was the idea of teaching chimps to use the sign language employed by the deaf. The most talkative among them have acquired vocabularies of a few hundred words, which they can assemble into rudimentary sentences. This enables the chimps to communicate on their own initiative, to make demands instead of merely obeying them. Parrots, who can mimic human sounds, are even better at learning words and putting those words together in a meaningful way. One famous parrot managed to acquire a vocabulary of over eight hundred words. Still, what chimps and parrots have to say when they learn a human language is of interest to us mainly because a parrot or a chimp is saying it. By human standards, their conversation is not exactly scintillating.

Because we tend to equate intelligence with language—particularly the ability to use language to think and communicate abstractions—it is natural to conclude that animals are, on the whole, a lot less intelligent than we are. We may imagine that without the medium of language it is impossible for them to share our spiritual concerns, or to comprehend our philosophical questions. We tend to conceive of animals as rather simple on a psychospiritual level, incapable of experiencing something like existential angst because they lack the vocabulary we use to make ourselves unhappy in that way. Since no animal has ever been heard to utter "to be or not to be" we figure they have nothing to say in response to that question.

Let's try looking at it another way. Maybe animals don't use language because they don't need to. They communicate and understand perfectly well without it. Indeed, from an animal's perspective, human words might just add ambiguity to a situation that would otherwise be clear. For instance, a human guardian may call "come" when wanting to feed a dog, or when wanting to give him a bath. Since the word might signal a desirable intention or an undesirable one, it is not, from the dog's point of view, very informative. The dog can better determine the human's intention by observing nonverbal cues or picking it up telepathically.

The same is often true of people. Even when we are chattering away at each other, 90 percent of the information is coming to us through something other than words: the speaker's facial expression, body language, tone of voice, and the context in which the words are being said. Say you encounter a coworker who is in danger of being laid off. In answer to "How's it going?" he says, "Couldn't be better." From his flat tone of voice, lack of eye contact, and what you know of his situation, you understand "Couldn't be better" to mean "I don't feel like talking about it." Now let's say that all of those cues are absent. You know nothing of the impending layoff. In response to your greeting, your coworker flashes a smile and says chirpily, "Couldn't be better." All of the obvious nonverbal clues are congruent with the words, yet you walk away with the feeling that your colleague is worried about something. You can't say why you have that feeling. Something just seems "off." What your coworker is at pains to conceal you are somehow picking up intuitively. In both of these cases, the words exchanged have been irrelevant. This may be why animals can't see the point of learning them. Animals are keenly interested in what people and other animals are feeling, and they trust what their senses and their intuition tell them. Insofar as human words are often *disinformation,* an animal can read a situation more accurately by ignoring them.

In human spiritual life, there are states of consciousness in which words drop away. Mystics are able to attain these states frequently and may report that words fail them when they attempt to describe what they have experienced. We regard these states as higher or more advanced than verbal intelligence. In pursuit of them, spiritual teachers will often exhort us to "quiet the mind." What they mean by that is to quiet the verbal center of the brain, to slow down or stop the incessant stream of words in our heads. Anyone who has ever attempted to do this knows what a major accomplishment it is. Animals, though, come by this inner stillness naturally. If to meditate is to stop talking to oneself, animals are meditating all the time. Imagine what they might have to teach us if we regarded them as our gurus!

For humans to take animals seriously as spiritual friends, partners, and even teachers, we would need to find a mode of communication with them that doesn't depend on language. Happily, such a mode exists. Both animals and humans are capable of sharing their thoughts and feelings intuitively, telepathically. Those people to whom we apply such condescending terms as "primitive" or "preindustrial" have always been able to do so, and it is common in their cultures to regard animals as spirit guides, divine messengers, or even as gods themselves. For humanity as a whole, this is nothing new, but in a world where people have lost track of the ability, it is rather startling. Animals have a lot to teach that people don't already know. I am most enthralled by what other creatures have to say when they are invited to wax philosophical. They have a great deal to tell us and were beginning to think we'd never ask.

You might be wondering how animals, who don't know human languages, manage to discourse about anything at all. What they transmit to the human listener is not words, but the meaning behind the words, the meaning that led people to invent a word in the first place. Think of what it's like when you're searching for a word you know, but have temporarily forgotten. You might say that the word is on the tip of your tongue, but no matter how hard you try, your tongue doesn't form it and your brain can't remember the sound of it. Still, you have a very specific word in mind, and no other word will do. What you actually have in mind is a concept, a meaning. And you find that you are perfectly capable of holding that meaning in your mind while you go on searching for the word. This is what it is like to receive an intuitive communication from someone, such as an animal, who doesn't use human language. The meaning arrives in your mind fully formed, and it is often quite specific. You then search your mind for the exact words that correspond to it. Because the meaning is so specific, you know when you've hit on the right words. Still the words are coming from your own brain. They are a translation into human language of a meaning that the animal transmitted wordlessly.

Mystics and mediums often describe exchanges with nonincarnate beings such as angels and deceased humans. Such reports are, I believe, no more and no less reliable than psychic connections with animals, in that the other party to the exchange is not in a position to contradict them. Mediums sometimes garble the message, and so do humans connecting with animals. Let's face it: if obliged to defend what we believe we have learned from an angel or an animal before a dissertation review committee, we would be stymied. A great many things that are worth knowing are ineligible for submission to an academic journal. I still want to know them, don't you?

I believe that everyone has the capacity to engage in telepathic communication. We are all born psychic. In many of us the ability remains latent, because we are not taught how to develop it or—worse—we are encouraged to suppress it. When we are very young, the people around us both validate and help us to interpret impressions coming through our physical senses by naming what we see, hear, taste, smell, and touch. If a person born deaf has her hearing restored by an operation, her newfound hearing is not of immediate use to her because she doesn't know how to interpret the sounds, how to distinguish one word from another, or how to differentiate talking from the roar of traffic and the hum of an air conditioner. The same is true of our psychic impressions. If no one around us acknowledges them and helps us to understand what they mean, they don't tell us anything useful, and we soon learn to ignore them. If—as is quite common—adults disparage our early psychic impressions as "just your imagination" we conclude that such experiences are better left unshared, lest we be branded as liars or just plain crazy. We learn to keep our psychic impressions a secret from others, and before long they have become a secret we keep from ourselves.

Yet few of us succeed in suppressing our intuitions entirely. When our worried coworker smiles and chirps "Couldn't be better" we sense that something is amiss. Though we might doubt that vague impression, we notice when we are getting it. Intuition doesn't stop working merely because we are mistrustful of it.

Russell Targ, a laser physicist with forty years of experience in psychic research, spent two decades working on government-supported investigations on ESP, through the Stanford Research Institute (SRI), which he cofounded with laser physicist Dr. Harold Puthoff in 1972. In his recent book, *The Reality of ESP,* Targ presents significant scientific research demonstrating that consciousness stretches far beyond the boundaries of our brains and bodies. He moves us beyond conventional barriers, examining our vast potential for nonlocal (outside of time and space) awareness. He believes ESP is an ability we all possess that becomes stronger by expanding our awareness to think nonlocally, and that it will become less mysterious as more of us develop these skills. He tells us that science defines the word *proof* as "overwhelming evidence, so strong, that it would be logically or probabilistically unreasonable to deny the supported argument. Proof establishes knowledge or the truth of a conclusion—such as aspirin preventing heart attacks, in which case the evidence was so strong that the National Institutes of Health stopped the experiments to avoid killing off the untreated controls." Targ states the evidence proving the existence of ESP, remote viewing, "has effect size ten times greater than aspirin." Based on the overwhelming amount of data proving ESP, he goes on to say, "I believe that we have completed our physical growth; our brains are big enough. I am proposing that transcending our own species is the next evolutionary step for us to take. . . . We are finally ready to meet our destiny as beings aware of our spacious and nonlocal consciousness, transcending space and time and accepting the gift of psychic abilities." He further states, "Our hardware is fine; it's our awareness of our psychic software that must be upgraded—and quickly, given the critical state of affairs. When we accomplish that, we will realize that, in consciousness, we are all one."

In her book, *Love, Life, and Elephants: An African Love Story,* Daphne Sheldrick tells us,

> Mysteriously . . . the ex-orphan elephants who are now living wild anticipate ahead of time the arrival (into the compound) of new nursery elephants. How they know this defies human interpretation, but it happens far too often to be chance. Mobile phone signals are poor in Tsavo's remote north, and there have been occasions when even the Ithumba keepers have been unaware that the new elephants are on their way, yet the independent ex-orphans are the "giveaway," turning up unexpectedly to wait at the stockade compound for the new arrivals. We can only assume that telepathy is at work, and, even more astoundingly, that such telepathy can only be between the ex-orphans and the Nairobi keepers, since there have been instances when new transferees are not known by those living wild. The reunions are always filled with a great outpouring of love.

Relationships with animals can be a great help to us in recovering and honing our inborn psychic ability. In one of his random telephone surveys, Rupert Sheldrake found that people who had cats or dogs were significantly more likely to report that they themselves had experienced telepathy. It is also important to note, as animals reawaken our psychic abilities, we naturally become more open-minded, letting go of old cultural taboos about psychic phenomena—allowing exciting possibilities in scientific inquiry to emerge. In his most recent book, *Science Set Free,* Sheldrake takes on ten dogmas of modern science and turns them into questions. One of the ten dogmas is that "unexplained phenomena such as telepathy are illusory." The question becomes, "Are psychic phenomena illusory?" With so much research now available, it is difficult to deny that telepathy, precognition, and other psychic phenomena are real. In my years of working with animals and their human companions, I find it difficult to come up with even a few instances where humans deny having had some type of psychic experience with their companion animal.

If you live with an animal, you know what it's like to have your feelings understood without your having to express them in words. You have also learned to sense what your animal feels and needs, and have been rewarded by a purr or a wagging tale for getting it right. Your cat never calls you crazy. Your dog never accuses you of imagining things. Animals are the most patient of teachers, and they are overjoyed when we make any attempt at all to perceive their inner life.

PART II

What Animals Want Us to Know

Chapter 3

YOU ARE LOVED

Love is the only reality and it is not a mere sentiment. It is the ultimate truth that lies at the heart of creation.

—RABINDRANATH TAGORE

I once spent thirty minutes or so at gunpoint. It was nothing personal. I was on a slow and crowded bus in Indonesia, trying to read, when an eruption of jabbering in the local language caused me to look up from my book. A passenger who had just boarded was engaged in a heated dispute with the driver. Since I didn't speak the language, I couldn't tell what the conflict was about. The jabbering continued as the bus started moving again and I went back to trying to read. Suddenly everyone around me was screaming. The irate passenger, still standing at the front of the bus, had pulled a gun. I remember wondering why the gun seemed to be aimed exactly in the direction of my forehead. The fight-or-flight response that could be expected under such circumstances didn't happen, perhaps because it was obvious from the outset that there was nothing I could do to ensure my survival. Having nothing to do was strangely calming. I considered the possibility that these were the final minutes of my life, and thought some summing-up was in order. What had been the point of that life? What had I loved most about it?

What immediately came to mind was a memory of riding my horse in the African bush. I was teaching school in Ghana at the time. Every afternoon when I got off work, I would rush to the stable, eager to be reunited with my equine friend. She was named Je t'aime, which means "I love you" in French. Most days I saddled her up, but on this occasion I just climbed on and rode bareback. I let her set the pace and lead the way over the rough trails meandering through the bush. Along the way, she would briefly turn and glance at me with one eye, reminding me she was paying attention for any snakes nearby; you didn't want to step too close to them, especially since in this part of Africa there were many poisonous ones. She would also pause and glance back to let me know when she was about to change her pace. Confident that Je t'aime knew what she was doing, I never worried about my safety. In silent communion, we would share with each other the emotions of our day, both of us taking a lot of deep, contented sighs.

The sky in Africa has always seemed bigger to me, more expansive and majestic than the skies anywhere else I have lived in the world. On this particular day it was especially breathtaking: a stunningly deep shade of blue. The sun, low on the horizon, cast a golden light over everything. The scent of the bush grasses swishing in the wind was like a tonic to me. I knew that Je t'aime, too, was immersed in this beauty. Briefly she paused, letting me know that she wanted to break into a run. Was that okay? I bent forward, clasping my arms around her neck. "Let her rip, girl!" I could feel the joy rippling through her body at this permission to do what came most naturally to her. She took off, her mane flying in the warm wind. Deafened by the thundering of her hooves, I could no longer hear the gentle rustling of the grasses or the hum of insects. The joy that surged through her filled my own body as well. It reached a pitch of ecstasy that threatened to overwhelm me.

In those moments of exaltation, I had the curious sensation of being able to see myself from the outside. It wasn't like being out of my body, for I was aware of the subtle muscular shifts in my body and in Je t'aime's as we effortlessly synchronized our movements. I was aware of our rapid breathing and of the pounding contact with the earth. I was totally in my body, yet able to witness it at the same time, because my senses had expanded to become one with the wind, the sun, the sky, and the Earth. There was no boundary, no place where I left off and the rest of the world began. I felt like I was made of champagne bubbles, and everything else was made of champagne bubbles, and the forces that run the universe had just uncorked the bottle with a celebratory pop. The moment expanded. Like the African sky, time itself became more capacious. It swelled with immense love until a minute became forever. I knew that love for a certainty, for I could feel it fizzing in my own bloodstream. And I knew for a certainty that Je t'aime was feeling it too. That moment of shared ecstasy sealed a soul bond between us that nothing in this world could ever break. It is the moment I chose to relive as I sat on the bus with a gun pointed at my head.

The bus pulled over to the side of the road and some men boarded, subdued the guy with the gun and hustled him off. By then I was feeling completely at peace, not because I was certain that the incident would conclude harmlessly, but because I felt like I would be okay no matter what the outcome. I had felt a divine love, and that love was everywhere, so if some crazy person took it on himself to relocate me with a bullet there was nothing to fear. Je t'aime herself had transitioned years ago, and our love for each other had held firm. Her spirit was there for me on that bus.

Riding Je t'aime is the closest I've ever come to the blissful union with the divine that mystics seek through meditation. I meditate regularly, have been doing so most of my adult life, and highly recommend it. But the greatest moments of spiritual opening don't usually happen then. Rather, meditation sows a seed of authentic presence with ourselves that explodes into spontaneous bloom, often when we least expect it. For me, these moments of awakening occur most often in relation to animals.

Many people believe that they ought to love God (in whatever form or whatever name they resonate with), but can't tell whether God is loving them back. When they attempt to pray or meditate, nothing much happens by way of divine response. A relationship with someone who seldom returns our calls is difficult to sustain. Religions have taught us to expect the response to come from above, but I believe it is actually much closer to the ground. What we have trouble apprehending with our minds comes to us through our senses. Everything in the created world is a manifestation of God's nature, the Source, love. You can hear the answer to your prayers in a chorus of starlings. You can hold God in your lap, feel God's heartbeat, and stroke God's fur. You can sense God's delight in you when you are greeted by a wagging tail. You can climb on God's back and go for a ride.

The Source of all expresses love by appearing to us in these loveable forms, forms that by their very nature open us to receiving love. When we believe ourselves to be undeserving of love—from our Source or from other people—our despondent hearts shut down and the message of love can't get in. But animals are capable of startling us into a state of receptivity. When a companion animal licks us or rubs against our leg or jumps into our lap, a rush of feel-good hormones reduces our stress level and tells our bodies that all is well. When we are amused by the antics of a squirrel, charmed by the singing of birds, or enchanted by the magical appearance of a dragonfly, our pleasure is as spontaneous and unself-conscious as the creature who evokes it. To ask whether we are worthy of this pleasure doesn't occur to us.

Contact with other creatures invites us into a world where human notions of deserving do not apply. Animals don't judge themselves to be sinful, unworthy, or inadequate. They don't lay such judgments on people either. Animals don't care how much you weigh, how smart you are, how much money you have, or what you are wearing. They don't care what you believe, or what you may have done wrong in your life. If you are good to them, you are good, period. Love is their sole standard of judgment.

Most people have heard the words "an elephant never forgets." What they never forget is love. Daphne Sheldrick tells us in *Love, Life and Elephants,*

The fact that elephants never forget has been proven to us time and time again, once by Eleanor in her forties, when she returned to the stockades after many years of wild living and a man who was a stranger to the incumbent keepers happened to be approaching from a distance. Up went Eleanor's trunk, her ears stood out, and much to everyone's alarm, she ran at speed toward the stranger, enveloping him with her trunk and treating him to a highly charged elephant greeting. It turned out that he had been her keeper when she was five years old, and even though thirty-seven years had passed since she had seen him last, her recognition was instant.

The Jesuit paleontologist Pierre Teilhard de Chardin wrote, "Love is the affinity which links and draws together the elements of the world." Love is how the world is made, and what the world is made of. To love an animal—and feel an animal loving you back—is to know this for sure.

Compassion for animals is the reaction of an open heart. The poet Rumi adored animals, as the following story describes. A young disciple noticed Rumi kept leaving his house with rich food, and he immediately thought the worst—that Rumi was going off to eat the food himself, secretly. One day, he followed Rumi to a ruined mosque outside the walls of Konya. There he saw Rumi feeding an exhausted, emaciated dog and her six newborn, starving pups. Noticing the young man, Rumi smiled and said, "When your heart is awake, you hear the cries of the animals from a long way off and you will come, and you will love, and administer unto them."

THANK YOU FOR LOVING ME

Someone found a small, stray dog and dropped him off at a clinic where I was working. The dog, who had probably been abandoned, had been fending for himself for quite some time, and was in bad shape. He had parasites and skin lesions, and one of his legs was misshapen from a leg fracture that had healed without being properly set. More worrying were the twitches that indicated the onset of distemper. The disease is contagious and regarded as incurable, so distempered animals are usually put to sleep. But something in this little guy's eyes begged me to give him a chance. I had read about an unconventional treatment—an off-label use of some medicine intended for a different condition—that I heard worked in a few cases. I decided to give it a try. To my delight, the dog rallied. Whenever I came into the room where I was keeping him in isolation, his tail wagged furiously. I dared to hope that he was cured. But after a week or so, he began to decline again, and it was obvious that he was not going to make it. Rather than put him to sleep, I tried to make the last days of his life happier than the rest of it had been. I spent a lot of time cuddling and playing with him, and when he finally died, it was in my arms. I will never forget the tender expression in his eyes as he looked up at me. They conveyed one simple message: "Thank you for loving me. I am grateful for this time we have shared. It has brought me comfort and healing."

Great teachers often come to us in humble packaging. That little dog held the wisdom of a sage in his heart. I learned from him that healing is not about the success or failure of the physical body, that physical survival is secondary. All creatures wish to live and thrive, but bodies do wear out. The number of days we walk the Earth (or fly or swim or crawl on it) is not the point. Animals live in the present moment. If kindness, caring, and respect fill that moment, life is full, no matter what came before or might come in the future. A soul that feels loved is joyous and healed.

An animal will often come into our lives at a moment when we need healing, or when we need to learn a lesson of love (which, from a divine perspective, is the same thing as needing to be healed). Stray cats and dogs, for instance, have a way of showing up and attaching themselves to people who don't think they want an animal companion, but need one. My favorite example of this is Hal, a huge hulk of a man who huffed into the clinic one day with a cardboard box. The previous evening he'd found it in a parking lot, sitting next to his car, with a note attached that read, "Please help me." Inside the box was a newborn white kitten. He described the incident with a kind of "last straw" exasperation, as one more hassle in a life that was apparently filled with hassles. But when he opened the box, the tenderness with which he lifted out the kitten belied his gruff tone.

He named the cat Snow because six inches of snow had fallen that night. Had he not rescued the kitten, she probably would not have survived. Over the years I became friends with both Hal and Snow and got to know them pretty well. The first time we met, Hal's life was imploding. His wife had just left him, he loathed his job, and the evident chip on his shoulder had rendered him pretty much friendless. He couldn't stand himself, or anyone else. Snow melted him. Having someone to take care of opened his heart and reconnected him with the world. Each time I saw him, he was a little bit softer, and more cheerful, and more in love with Snow. He finally quit his job and moved to Arizona, which he had wanted to do for a long time. The cat he had so grudgingly rescued had ended up rescuing him.

In Cincinnati, there is a residential center for the mentally ill homeless people called Tender Mercies. A friend and I used to visit regularly, bringing a few small animals with us. Residents called us "the pet club." They mostly ignored us and talked to the animals instead. I remember one resident in particular—a tall, thin, and androgynous young man named Andy. He wore men's clothes with women's accessories and lipstick. Usually Andy was very withdrawn, but the day I brought a rabbit and let him take it into his lap, it was as if someone had plugged him in. With great animation, he talked about a pet rabbit he'd had when he was a little boy. Suddenly you could see that boy, the happy, outgoing child he had been before life had beaten him up and driven him inward.

Princess Diana once said, "The biggest disease today is the feeling of being unwanted. Without love, people die." Her own story demonstrates that we can have everything, yet be starving on the inside.

As a child, I felt unwanted. My father, who worked long hours, wasn't around much, and my only sibling was much older than I was. For reasons I never fully understood, my mother was emotionally unavailable to me. The messages I got from her were all about my deficiencies. I was a quiet, inward, awkward child, so slow to start talking that once I overheard my parents wondering whether I was deaf. I could hear just fine, but what people said in words didn't seem very interesting to me, and I had nothing to add to it. I was also extremely thin and self-conscious about it. Even in the heat of the summer, I wore sweaters to hide my meager arms. The scantiness of my body seemed expressive of my overall feeling of insufficiency.

That feeling went away whenever I was in the backyard on my own. I paid close attention to what went on there, especially the doings of the various creatures—the birds and bugs and other small animals. I began to recognize some of them as individuals. The more I paid attention, the more they communicated their individuality to me. At the same time, I noticed the relationships various creatures were having with each other. It was as if they were all members of a big, friendly club. It seemed to me that the attention was mutual, that these other creatures were aware of me, and warmly accepting of my presence. I couldn't seem to make the cut in the human club, but they welcomed me into theirs.

In a way, animals raised me. I was imprinted by them, by their reality, at a young age. The memories of the experiences I had in nature with them, all the things they taught, remain fixed inside, forever part of me. They taught me their language, which I seemed to understand better than human language. They taught me how to make friends and sustain relationships, and instilled in me the confidence of belonging somewhere. Unless we are recognized by another, we don't know who we are. The animals taught me who I was. It is not something I can put a name to in human words, even now. But watching a ladybug crawl over a leaf, or mirroring the tilted head of a curious bird with my own tilted head, I felt "this is me" and this "me" was sufficient after all. I believe that my backyard companions sensed my loneliness, that they saw me as a young animal in need of adoption and responded to my need.

ANIMAL BODHISATTVAS

It is not uncommon for animals to respond to the needs of young ones—including humans—outside their own species. A few children owe their lives to this phenomenon.

In Tanganyika, a native woman had placed her sleeping baby in the shade of tree. Suddenly there was a crash in the brush as a herd of elephants passed by. When they noticed the child, they stopped, pulled some branches from the tree and tenderly covered it, careful not to wake it. The game-preserve worker who witnessed this believed that the elephants were trying to shade the infant from the sun.

At the Brookfield Zoo in Chicago, a toddler somehow got away from his mother and fell twenty feet into the pit surrounding the gorilla enclosure, where he lay unconscious. A female gorilla hurried over to him, picked him up, and cradled him in her arms, using her body to shield him from the other apes. Then she carried him to the door used by the zookeepers, set him down beside it, and guarded him until he could be rescued by humans. Amazingly, this was not the first such incident. At another zoo, ten years earlier, a child who had fallen into the ape enclosure was rescued by a male gorilla.

Some of the most popular videos on YouTube feature domestic animals who have adopted orphans from other species: cats nursing puppies or rabbits, dogs adopting cats or monkeys, and so forth. Even stranger pairings have occurred in zoos and wildlife sanctuaries: a sheep adopting a baby elephant, a Bengal tiger caring for orphaned piglets, and a sow adopting baby tigers. In many of these cases, the match has been encouraged by human caretakers to console a mother who has lost her own young. But oddball adoptions have also been documented in the wild. A young antelope who became separated from its herd was adopted by a lioness. A baby hippopotamus who lost her mother in the 2004 tsunami bonded with a giant tortoise.

One story of interspecies adoption is so outlandish that few people would believe it had it not been captured on film. A documentary crew was following a young female leopard when she happened upon a female baboon who had become temporarily separated from her group. Taking advantage of the baboon's isolation, the leopard killed her. As she began to feed on the carcass, she discovered a newborn, still clinging to its mother's lifeless body. Fascinated, she stopped feeding to examine the little creature. Gently she picked it up with her mouth and carried it up to a tree branch, to keep it safe. There she continued to examine and play with it for some minutes until a hyena showed up, attracted by the smell of blood. The leopard bravely fended off the hyena, not in defense of her kill (which she appeared to have forgotten about) but in defense of the baby baboon. She kept the infant with her for the rest of the day and all through the night when, sadly, it died of exposure.

It is commonplace in our time to explain the behavior of all living creatures—humans as well as animals—in Darwinian terms. In this rather dispiriting view, adjectives like *noble* and *compassionate* do not apply. Behaviors that appear to be altruistic are nothing more than an expression of the instinct to ensure the survival of the species. What the theory cannot adequately explain are acts of interspecies kindness. Humans and other animals will sometimes go to great lengths to help a creature in trouble without stopping to ask "What's in it for me?" or "What's in it for my species?" Insofar as care for the young, the vulnerable, and the endangered is a survival instinct, it transcends the boundaries of species. Living creatures instinctively want to perpetuate *life itself*. In some cases, this instinct to protect life itself even trumps the pursuit of individual or group survival. An animal will put its own life at risk to protect some creature it would normally regard as prey.

To be sure, such cases are exceptional. Among animals, as among humans, there exist saints and bodhisattvas: individuals who have out-stripped their fellows in spiritual development. A compassionate pig or gorilla or leopard, like a compassionate human, demonstrates the highest potential of its species. The presence of animal bodhisattvas reminds us that altruism isn't unique to humans. All living creatures possess the capacity to feel and act out of selfless love.

It has been my great, good fortune to know one of these animal saints personally. His name was Wimsey. He first entered my life in Ghana, as a stray kitten who had gotten his head stuck in a small can of evaporated milk. As soon as I rescued him from this ignominious predicament, our eyes met. It was mutual love at first sight. That night I settled him in a little basket on the floor, then got into bed myself. Immediately he sprang out of the basket and clawed his way up the bedclothes (he was too small to jump) to lie beside me. When I put him back in the basket, he did it again. In all, I made five or six attempts to insist on the basket before giving in to his even greater insistence on sleeping in my bed. Wimsey knew better than I knew myself that curled up against me was where I needed him to be.

For the next eighteen years, Wimsey was my friend and traveling companion. Indeed, he was often the only constant during that itinerant and tumultuous period in my life. On international flights, he accompanied me into the passenger cabin. I considered this his due, for I never conceived of him as a pet. He was my equal, my soulmate, and at times even my teacher. A shaman once told me that I was lucky to have such an evolved being in my life. This I already knew. Wimsey was a master meditator, a wise soul, a feline Gandhi. He enjoyed watching birds with me, restraining his instinct to pounce. In the various menageries that I called home over the years, he played host to the ever-changing population of orphaned pets and rescued wildlife, making newcomers welcome, comforting the traumatized, mediating conflicts, and keeping everyone organized and calm, including me.

During the final days of his life, as he was succumbing to chronic kidney failure, he could no longer make it up the stairs to my bedroom, so we slept together on the dining room floor. On his last day of life, I sat with him in my lap, neither of us moving for several hours, until he peacefully left his body. That day happened to be my daughter's fifth birthday. I remember thinking how bizarre it was that he would die on that of all days. Then during the night I received a message from him, during a dream. He had chosen that day on purpose. He knew how deeply I loved my daughter and wanted me to know that I was not alone, that she would still be there for me.

THE DARK SIDE OF LOVE

If you are open to receiving spiritual teachings from animals at all, it is natural to expect them to come from those who are innately impressive: lions, elephants, eagles, and such. But a squirrel? Their antics are fun to watch, yet squirrels are so common that I, like most people, don't pay them much attention. So it came as a big surprise to me when a squirrel taught me one of the most valuable lessons in my life.

Late one afternoon, I was out walking with two friends, chatting with them as we took a familiar route through our quiet, suburban neighborhood. Suddenly, out of nowhere, a beagle pup darted into the road, about three blocks ahead of where we were. At the same moment, we heard a woman's scream. The dog was almost safely across when a car struck it and drove on. I ran to the scene, hoping to administer first aid but reached the dog just in time to see him gasp his last breath. There was nothing to do but to close his eyes and wait with the woman until her husband arrived.

That night I lay awake, consumed with rage. Had I, with all my veterinary training, fortuitously been near enough to witness the accident and treat the injured beagle, I would have seen it as a gesture of divine providence. I would have believed that my presence at the scene was meant to be. But what was the point of my being there when I was helpless to prevent the accident or save the dying dog? My proximity to the scene was, as far as I could see, nothing but a cruel and meaningless coincidence. What purpose had been served by it, other than to add my suffering to that of the woman and her puppy? The bottom fell out of my faith. Life struck me that night as heartlessly absurd.

Over the next few days, the underlying question—"What is the point?"—continued to fester, unresolved and seemingly unresolvable. I was still in a deep funk over it when a bizarre reenactment of the traumatic event unfolded. I was driving on a two-lane thoroughfare not far from home, a road frequented at that hour by commuters, many of them distracted and driving too fast. Just ahead, I saw a full-grown gray squirrel bolt out into the road, straight into the path of a speeding SUV. The driver either didn't notice that he'd hit the animal or didn't think the life of a squirrel worth stopping for. I slammed on the brakes and ran to the scene. Once again, I hoped to offer professional assistance, and once again I found the animal to be injured beyond saving. When I reached him, he flipped his dying body up and toward me to make sure I saw his face. His purpose in this came through to me very clearly, for turning over took the last of his remaining energy, and there was no other reason for him to do it. He fixed his eyes on me very intently, as if insisting, "Look!" Our gazes locked. I can't remember a time when I saw God more clearly expressed in a face.

Frozen in that moment, we connected. I got it. What I saw, reflected back to me in the eyes of the dying squirrel was the power of my own presence in that moment. It was immensely more powerful than I had ever imagined. The reason for my presence was simply that—to be there at the moment of another's death, to witness it and to care.

When I was a little girl, I used to imagine a sort of animal sanctuary in heaven. It was a vast expanse of sky where animals who had died, or were alone, or abandoned, could run or fly or swim in never-ending freedom and delight. I called it "Rainbow Bend." Some seers report that there exist actual heavens created by the human imagination, that what we envision vividly and repeatedly becomes an independent reality that can be perceived and occupied by others. I like to think that this is true, that all my years of imagining it have actually built a paradise for my abandoned and departed animal friends, and that, with my help, the dying squirrel went straight to Rainbow Bend. From a veterinary perspective, there was nothing to be done for him. But from God's perspective and that of a dying creature, there is always something to be done, for simply being present is doing something. On a spiritual level, to be present is the *main* thing to be done, and if you are placed at the scene of some hardship you can't fix, it is because your presence—your *particular* presence—is wanted. That's what the dying squirrel taught me. It was a difficult and important lesson for a vet to learn.

I take it hard when an animal in my care suffers or dies. I take it even harder when the animal's suffering is the result of human exploitation or carelessness. For much of my life, I judged this to be a weakness in myself. My greatest fear was that I might someday collapse from it, find myself so prostrate with grief and outrage that I would be incapable of functioning. Sometimes the mere anticipation of this collapse tempted me to give up my work before it could occur. I told myself that I lacked the requisite toughness for animal work in general, and for endangered-animal rescue in particular.

What I most feared eventually came to pass. It was every bit as bad as I had imagined. I was at the time a veterinary consultant for an animal-rescue organization in Southeast Asia. One day I got an urgent call about an intercepted shipment of smuggled hyacinth macaws.

Hyacinths are the largest bird of the parrot family—about three feet long on average—and one of the most beautiful creatures on Earth. Their plumage is an electric shade of blue, a blue so vivid and intense that you can hardly believe your eyes. As an endangered species, hyacinths can't be legally exported or sold, but they fetch a high price on the black market. As is often the case, the smuggled hyacinths had been stuffed into ordinary suitcases, checked on a commercial flight. Smugglers take it for granted that some of the birds will likely suffocate under these conditions and, rather, illogically, cram in as many of them as possible. They figure that if at least one or two survive, the trip will have been sufficiently profitable.

I'd been told there were a dozen birds, and expected to find them in varying degrees of distress. As I rushed to the clinic, I was already creating a plan in my mind. I imagined the anxious bustle I would encounter upon my arrival and pictured how I would respond, for time was of the essence, and to work efficiently would be imperative. Like a soldier heading to the front lines, I donned an armor of steely determination. But when I burst through the clinic door, I was greeted by an ominous silence. People were standing around motionless, with stunned looks on their faces. For a moment I felt entirely disoriented. Then a sense of horror crept over me as I realized what the eerie stillness was about. We were too late. Twelve hyacinths, in all their aching beauty, lay lifeless on the floor.

Next thing I knew, I was on the floor with them, felled by a wave of grief and rage too powerful for my body to withstand. My head spun and my legs buckled under me. My chest felt blown open, as if a grenade had exploded there. I broke into ungovernable sobbing, past caring what a spectacle I was making of myself. Yet no matter how hard I cried, I couldn't seem to release the grief. It was bottomless. For every tear I shed, another ten welled up. I despaired of ever weeping my way to the end of them.

It went on for a long time. Days turned to weeks in which vast stretches of bleak despair were punctuated by storms of weeping that exhausted me without bringing any comfort or relief. I have known people who committed suicide because they couldn't bear to live in such a dark world, and I began to think I might become one of them. To help animals seemed the only thing worth doing with my life, and I was clearly incapable of it. I couldn't save the hyacinths and I was in no fit state to save anything else. The lid of the smuggler's suitcase had snuffed out the meaning in my life, and I was suffocating in a heap of blue feathers.

In his book *The Hope*, Andrew Harvey recounts the suicide of a friend who had devoted her life to working with indigenous peoples threatened by the destruction of the Amazon rain forest. In a letter to him shortly before her death, she had written, "The very thing that drove me to do my work—my conscience—has become an unendurable agony to me. In a world descending into barbarism, having a conscience is like having leprosy; it eats you away. Forgive me. I cannot bear the pain of loving the world anymore."

What shocked Harvey most about her suicide was that her deep spirituality and altruistic love of the world had not protected her from despair, but had in fact been the *cause* of that despair. His belief that his own spiritual life would render him immune to suicidal feelings was shaken, and within weeks he found himself teetering on the same precipice. He writes:

> I began the morning calm and focused, but after two hours of reading about polluted landscapes, ruined rivers, and the deaths of thousands of innocent villagers (while fat-cat CEOs were drinking champagne in Lagos), I began to feel sick to my stomach. I thought I needed some air, so I walked out onto Lexington Avenue.
>
> I stood on the sidewalk, suddenly invaded by the mad noise of city traffic hurtling past, by the cold horror of what I had been reading. For one blinding moment, all I wanted was to step out into the traffic and be run over. It took all the strength I had to restrain myself.

He goes on to say that he is now grateful for that moment, not only because it helped him share in his friend's pain, but because it forever ended his belief that spirituality would render him invulnerable to such feelings.

If you do not accept that facing this ferocity will bring you to your knees in despair and drive you to wish you had never been born, you will never be able to find the authentic hope that is born when you offer up this heartbreak to the Beloved for Him to heal and steady, and so discover that you can bear it without denial and continue to love life. . . . It is our most frightening fragilities that can lead us, if we are humble and lucid enough to work with them, to our most reliable sources of strength. Until I had faced the fact that the work I had chosen to do could drive me to suicide or threaten my sanity, I was in danger from my own unacknowledged shatteredness that I papered over with bravura and rhetoric.

You might be hoping to hear that my despair finally resolved itself in a moment of deep consolation. That didn't happen. All I could find by way of comfort was a tiny point of light, a pinprick of light so faint it wouldn't even have been perceptible if not surrounded by utter darkness. The light was inviting me closer, held no judgment, simply beckoned me to keep moving toward it despite my anguish. And I discovered that I could do so.

That light was the love of what I will call God, in front of me, inviting me in and offering to hold my pain. I kept my eyes on it, kept following it until it led me to a place that was beyond anger, beyond the egoic desire to escape. It took a great deal of time, but eventually I came to understand that I could experience the worst despair imaginable, the despair I had been dreading all my adult life, and keep going. My deep love and compassion for animals, which I thought my greatest weaknesses, were in fact, my greatest strengths, my gifts. Shutting down the love in my heart was simply not an option. I discovered that prayer isn't about asking for things to be different. It's about asking to be shown the blessing that is *within* the pain.

Nietzsche was right when he wrote, "Whatever doesn't kill me makes me stronger." I came to fully understand that my capacity for anguish was not a weakness, but a blessing. It was the shadow side of my capacity for love. The love came from the same bottomless place the tears came from. Grief and outrage were not, as I had always supposed, the obstacles to my calling. They were the *expression* of that calling. Once I realized this, I knew I would never again collapse in hopelessness. Sorrow would never again knock me off my feet. From now on, sorrow would be what held me upright.

The depth of loss people feel when a companion animal dies is hard for those who don't live with animals to fathom. Compared to the loss of a spouse or a parent or a child, the death of a dog or cat may seem trivial, but many people mourn long and hard when it happens. The grief is especially poignant because the loss is so pure, the love between human and animal so simple and unambivalent. People will say of their departed animal, "I have lost my best friend" or "I have lost the one who loved me most in this world." When we love an animal, we do so with the innocence of a child, and when we lose that animal, we grieve like a child.

Paradoxically, the love of an animal activates a very adult place in us. We are aware that the manmade world is full of dangers for animals and that they are depending on us for protection. They depend on our being reliable and responsible, for if we are forgetful, they are helpless to do anything about their own hunger or thirst or loneliness. They depend, too, on our emotional steadiness, for if we are moody, cross, or cruel, they feel it as a small child would feel it. The part of our love that comes from this responsible, protective place is fierce. It has claws and a loud roar. It reacts out of all proportion to whatever it perceives as a threat to the beloved. A great many of those threats come from other humans—not so much from their deliberate cruelty as from carelessness and cluelessness. Loving one animal opens our hearts to the predicaments of all animals. When we realize how exploitive and inhospitable human civilization is from an animal point of view, our claws come out. We can't help it. Our rage is instinctive, ferocious, and devastating to experience.

When love cracks us open like this, leaving us more vulnerable than we think we can stand, the temptation to shut down, to lock up our hearts and throw away the key is fierce. In our spiritual lives, this is the moment of truth, the moment when we either retreat to safety or step forward to claim the vastness and terror of our full capacity to love. I will let the poet Rumi have the last word on this subject, for he says it better than I can.

> The grapes of my body can only become wine
> After the winemaker tramples me.
> I surrender my spirit like grapes to his trampling
> So my innermost heart can blaze and dance with joy.
> Although the grapes go on weeping blood and sobbing,
> "I cannot bear any more anguish, any more cruelty!"
> The trampler stuffs cotton in his ears: "I am not
> Working in ignorance.
> You can deny me if you want, you have every excuse,
> But it is I who am the Master of this Work.
> And when through my Passion you reach Perfection,
> You will never be done praising my name."

Chapter 4

YOU ARE ALREADY
LIVING IN PARADISE

All the animals except for man know that the principal business of life is to enjoy it.

—SAMUEL BUTLER

Maybe the title of this chapter dismays you. To say that we are already living in paradise suggests that we have nothing better to look forward to, that what we've already got is as good as it gets. Maybe you have not, to date, been under the impression that what we've got is all that good. In the world as you know it, there seems to be plenty of room for improvement.

Animals encounter plenty of adversity and often have even less power than humans have over conditions that threaten them or cause them pain. Like we do, they feel grief, anger, and fear. Nevertheless, they experience the world as fundamentally good, and their existence in it as basically happy. Joy is their default emotion, the constant sun behind every passing cloud. The animals I hear from are well aware that this is not how most humans feel. They perceive us as unique among creatures in our propensity for feeling unhappy. It bothers them—partly because they feel compassion for us, and partly because humans who can't see that the world is already paradise keep messing it up with misguided renovations. For their own sake, as well as for ours, the animals would like to help us to feel better.

THE PARADISE PERSPECTIVE

Has it ever struck you as odd that humans are the only creatures on the planet who wear clothes? All other beings, from aardvarks to zebras, are running around in their birthday suit, blissfully unclear on the concept of underpants. Why don't people do the same?

The Bible addresses this question very early on, in the Book of Genesis. According to Genesis, the world God made on Earth was the best of all possible worlds for everyone in it, including people. The only thing its inhabitants were forbidden to do was to eat the fruit growing on one particular tree, because it was infected with something that would make the eater miserable. The animals took God's word for it and left the fruit alone, but humans, being curious, wanted to find out what would happen if they broke the rule. Human clothing was the earliest symptom that the forbidden fruit was causing severe indigestion. Under its influence the eaters were, for the first time, able to look at themselves from the outside. As soon as they did so, they concluded that they looked really weird, and felt embarrassed.

From God's perspective, there was nothing at all wrong with the way people looked. The wrongness was in how they were doing the looking. In order to look at yourself from the outside, you have to mentally divide into two different selves: the one looking and the one being seen. Being divided in two doesn't feel right, and when you don't feel right, nothing looks right. To be "driven out of paradise" was not a physical event: that is, humans were not transported to some new and less desirable address. They remained in the same delightful world that God provided for them, but no longer experienced it as delightful because they were no longer looking at it from a wholesome perspective.

Genesis is a story about the origin of a spiritual problem. As an explanation of how the humans and everything else came into *physical* existence, it leaves a lot to be desired. In fact, it expresses a fundamental misunderstanding about Creation, because it was written subsequent to the perceptual shift it recounts. Once people developed the unfortunate knack for looking at themselves from the outside, regarding themselves as separate and self-contained units, they began to see everything else the same way. They focused on the various objects in the world, and paid little attention to the space between the objects, which they assumed to be empty and uninteresting.

Since the world appears to be full of physical things, it was natural for people to assume that it was made of something physical—i.e., matter. They figured that the large units of matter that they perceived as objects were assembled out of smaller units. For a long time, the smallest unit anyone knew of was the atom. Then physicists discovered that atoms are made of even finer particles. It turns out that these subatomic particles are so infinitesimally small and so sparsely concentrated that they occupy only about 0.0000000000000000000042 of the space in the universe. All the matter units on Earth would, if you squeezed out the space between, result in a pellet about the size of a pea. If the so-called "material world" were sold in a supermarket, they wouldn't even have to list matter as one of the ingredients on the Nutrition Facts label. Whether even this scant sprinkling of matter firmly exists is questionable, for upon closer inspection it seems to flicker on and off like fireflies on a summer evening. At this point, physicists will only say cautiously that matter has "a *tendency* to exist."

The negligible amount of matter that tends to exist in the universe appears to us as rocks and trees and bodies because it is coming together in an organized and purposeful way. Between the photons that make up a beam of light or the atoms that make up a rock is some kind of intelligent relatedness. This relatedness is very stretchy, for in proportion to the size of subatomic particles, the distance between them in an atom is the equivalent of thousands of miles. Yet an atom particle somehow "knows" that it belongs with its brother and sister particles and doesn't go hurtling off at random toward some other galaxy. As far as physicists have been able to tell, this knowing resides not in the particles themselves, but in what is between them. The space between isn't filled with anything physical, yet neither is it entirely empty. It has some quality of intelligent relatedness that might be described as consciousness.

This probably isn't the first time you've encountered a discussion of quantum physics in a book about spirituality. In chapter two, I mentioned the work of physicist Russell Targ and his book, *The Reality of ESP*. In it he quotes the physicist Henry Stapp of the Lawrence Berkeley National Laboratory who states, "What a person chooses to do in one region seems immediately to affect what is true elsewhere in the universe. This nonlocal aspect can be understood by conceiving the universe to be not a collection of tiny bits of matter, but rather a growing compendium of "bits of information." People who meditate a lot, or who study Buddhist, Hindu, or Taoist metaphysics, have always believed what physicists are belatedly discovering, and can seldom resist the urge to say, "I told you so." When mystics assert that the Source of all life is everywhere, this is what they are talking about. What we are used to calling the "material world" and the "spiritual world" are made of the same stuff: the mind of the Source, and we are all in this one mind together. Divine consciousness is built in to every cell, molecule, atom and subatomic particle. This is self-evident if you are looking at the world as the Source intends it to be seen: that is, from the perspective of that Source within you. Mystics describe it really well by telling us to imagine a bucket of water scooped from the ocean sitting on the shore. It seems separate, but it is still made up of the ocean. An individual wave, seemingly separate as it rushes to the shore, is still completely made up of the ocean and recedes back into it as one.

When you hear the expression "the God within" you might get a mental picture of yourself as a kind of container. Finding God must be a matter of removing the lid and peering inside. So you try removing the lid of that which you call "I" and inspect the contents of your soul, finding there a jumble of thoughts and feelings that don't strike you as in any way divine. The reason this doesn't work is that the self is once again divided in two. The looker is disconnected from that which is being looked at, so nothing looks right.

Let me offer you a visualization that might work better. Imagine that you (by "you," I mean your attention) are entering your body by way of your windpipe. Once inside your lung, you begin to become aware that it is made of individual cells. Close up, what appeared to be a solid wall of tissue is more like a dance of these loose individual cells moving around in space. Then you notice that the walls of the cells are permeable, so you decide to step inside one of them. You thought you were entering something much smaller than your lung, but for some reason, the inside of the cell feels much *larger*. Now you can see distinct molecules, and these are permeable too. You enter one and find that, from inside, it is even more spacious than the cell. You have discovered a world where the smaller something appears from the outside, the bigger it is on the inside. This curious reversal of how you expect the physical world to work enchants you. It is the first intimation that what you have always expected might be all wrong.

Gradually you become aware that there are a few atoms floating around in the room. They are so small and so sparsely distributed that at first you hardly noticed them, but as you move toward one of them, it grows much larger—big enough to let you inside. And once you're in, you discover that it is even more spacious than the inside of the molecule. It's so vast and empty that, if you'd thought of it ahead of time, you would have imagined that to be inside of it would make you feel terribly lost and lonely and insignificant. But this chamber, though physically empty, feels suffused with something like hospitality. It actively welcomes you, enveloping you in a warm embrace. It's as if the space is saying, "We're thrilled that you've finally come in." There is also something very lively about it, something intelligent and playful and humorous—an effervescent quality that makes you feel a bit giddy.

Think of the feeling you get when something you desire very much is about to happen in the very next moment, but hasn't happened yet. You're in a four-star restaurant and the most appetizing entrée you can imagine has just been placed before you, and you are picking up your fork to take the first bite. Or you have just settled yourself comfortably in your favorite chair and turned to the first page of a new book by your favorite author. Each inner space you enter is pregnant with some delicious possibility that is just on the verge of happening.

Like space, time in this new world is very stretchy. The more joy there is in a moment, the more that moment expands to let you take in your fill. It's as if your body were made of bubble wrap. Each bubble is an endlessly expandable moment of joy, and there are trillions of them. You are heir to an inexhaustible pleasure palace that is yours to explore whenever you like.

As you are luxuriating in the bliss of this discovery, you become aware that the bubble you are in is moving. It is hurtling through space with a speed you find totally exhilarating. The atom that was in your lung is being breathed out. It goes on flying through the air until it gets breathed in by a bird. You can tell that this has happened because the atmosphere of the bubble has become somehow birdlike. The atmosphere is singing and soaring. Being inside a bird is so much fun that you want to stay forever.

Then you feel a kind of jolt, a moment of inexplicable panic. You don't know what's happening, but it is scary, and you want to struggle against it. You do struggle a moment and then, just as suddenly, the fear passes. You feel a swooning sensation, as if you were falling backward onto a featherbed. The atmosphere shifts again, in a way that makes you realize that you are in the presence of a large and powerful cat. The cat has stunned the bird, and is about to feast on it. Though you feel like you *are* the bird, being eaten by the cat doesn't trouble you in the least. On the contrary, a tingle of joyous anticipation draws you toward the cat, as if getting eaten were the most seductive possibility in the world. Eagerly you move into the cat's mouth and as soon as you do, you find yourself in a space where the cat's consciousness and the bird's overlap, so that you can experience both at the same time. Your cat-self is finding your bird-self really yummy: you taste of soaring and singing. Bird-self feels proud of tasting so good, and honored to contribute to the nourishment of the magnificent creature that is cat-self. Upon finishing the meal, cat-self stretches lazily to bask in the sun, feeling replete and grateful. When she falls asleep, she dreams that she is flying.

What you are experiencing is the mind of God, divine consciousness, as it creates the world. The creating of the world is the greatest show on Earth, and you have the best seat in the house. This is the paradise within you. Animals live in what I call the Source or Great Spirit. It is what they and all the other creatures on Earth are so ridiculously happy about.

WHY HUMANS ARE NOT SO HAPPY

At the risk of dismaying you again, I want to talk about why, on the whole, animals are happier than people. It's a delicate subject, and often devolves into that flaky sort of nature romanticism that wants humans to become "noble savages" and run around naked in the woods. That's not where I'm going with this, so please bear with me. What I want to talk about is the glimpse of "paradise perspective" you just got, and why it's so different from a human's ordinary state of mind.

Imagine that you are lost in a densely wooded wilderness area. Though you have a map of the area, it isn't helping because the map is an overview and you can't figure out how it corresponds to what you're seeing at ground level. If there is a high hill or mountain nearby, you might try climbing to the top of it. With any luck, the view from above will resemble what you see on the map, enabling you to get your bearings. In essence, what you are doing is using an abstract representation of the area to solve a problem you are having in that area. This is a very human thing to do. As an approach to navigation and other sorts of practical problem solving, it works well for us.

We often take the same approach to our emotional or spiritual difficulties—attempting to distance ourselves from what's bothering us in order to understand it better. Say you are going through a painful breakup. It isn't the first such break-up, and when you step back and take an overview of your life, you may see it as part of a pattern. The discovery of this pattern makes you think you're onto something. By generalizing based on the pattern, you might discover what all the breakups have in common. By standing outside yourself, you might be able to see what you have been doing wrong. Or say you are wrestling with one of the big metaphysical questions, such as "What is the purpose of human existence?" or "What is the meaning of suffering?"

In your imagination, you project yourself outside of your immediate situation in order to gain an overview—that is, to see the Big Picture.

In theory, this sounds like it ought to work. In practice, though, it usually just makes us more confused, and more unhappy. When we disconnect from ourselves in order to see ourselves better, or disconnect from the world around us in order to understand it better, what we end up seeing is distorted by the disconnection itself. It's like unplugging an appliance and then wondering why it doesn't work.

Take the cat devouring the bird. If we regard what's happening from the outside, we feel sorry for the bird. As we see it, the cat is getting its nourishment at the bird's expense. In the competition for survival, the cat is the winner and the bird is the loser. We have a big objection to what's happening that the bird herself doesn't share, because the bird is connected. She is *having* her experience rather than watching and judging her experience. That experience, while fleetingly scary, climaxes in a moment that is as happy for the bird as it is for the cat. Being connected, the bird partakes of the cat's enjoyment.

It used to be thought that animals couldn't stand apart from their experience and pass judgment on it because they weren't conscious of being individual selves—that is, they couldn't really distinguish "I" from other. But even the most casual observation of animals shows us that they are capable of telling each other apart, that they choose their mates, mourn the loss of friends and family, and even sometimes make enemies demonstrates that they perceive individual differences to the extent of forming preferences. The individual bird knows that she is not the cat, and that she is not the cat's nest-mate. Animals don't experience themselves as glommed together in some amorphous "group soul" any more than we do.

It is not some undifferentiated "Oneness" that makes getting eaten by a cat acceptable to the bird. It is rather that the bird doesn't conceive of her self-ness in isolation from other selves. She doesn't picture herself standing there all alone as a self-contained unit. Rather the sense of "selfness" awakens *in relation* to other. Selfness is experienced at the point of connection with something else. Only when eaten by the cat does the bird discover how delicious she is.

"Uncle" Bob Randall, an aboriginal elder from Australia, likes to tell a story about a friend of his who happened to be a crocodile. The croc used to hang around in the water next to the pier where Bob liked to sit, and they would commune telepathically. One day, when Bob was thinking about how much he loved this crocodile, he heard him reply, "Yes you love me, but I love you even more, because if you ever fall into the water, you will be my supper." Bob just laughed. He understood that the croc didn't mean it in a sarcastic way. The croc was proposing an arrangement that he considered to be a win/win.

We humans tend to conceive of our consciousness as residing in the head, isolated from the minds of others by the hard container of the skull. We tend to assume that our own intelligence, and that of other creatures, is limited by the size and capabilities of the brain. For animals, intelligence is more like a medium through which they move. The intelligence of fish isn't limited to their rather limited brain capacity. Much of their knowing comes from the water. For earthworms, knowing comes from the soil. All of the elements—water, air, earth, light—are highly intelligent and inform consciousness both on the inside of the body and at every point of contact between the body and the external world. When we have an intuition—that is, when we "just know" something without being able to put our finger on *how* we know it—this is where the information is coming from. We take in intelligence with every breath. We absorb it through the sun on our skin and the earth under our feet. It washes over us whenever we take a shower. When informed by this elemental intelligence, our perceptions are accurate and our decisions are sound. It is only when we attempt to think in isolation from it that we start to make mistakes.

It is commonplace, and true, to point out that animals are happier than people because they live entirely in the present. Yet to say this to people is also rather annoying, since they can't really see what use to make of the information. Humans conceive of time, like matter, as being divided into units—weeks, hours, minutes. If you take a minute, and picture yourself at the exact center of it, the first thirty seconds are in the past, and the next thirty seconds are in the future. Even a nanosecond can be divided in this way. So when spiritual teachers tell you that the secret of happiness is living in the present, you can be forgiven for wondering "*What* present?"

The reason animals find it easier than we do to live in the present is that their present is longer than ours. Let me give you an example of what I mean. My dear friend David, who died recently, used to have a Labrador retriever called Bodhi. Each evening when David returned home from work, Bodhi would go nuts with joy, leaping up and down, standing on his hind legs to lick David's face, running around in circles, then leaping up to lick some more. Once Bodhi settled down, David would leave the house again to collect his mail from the box at the end of the driveway. Upon his return Bodhi would reenact the entire greeting ritual just as exuberantly. The fact that David had only been away for five minutes didn't dilute Bodhi's enthusiasm in the slightest. Every homecoming was, for Bodhi, a cause for the most elaborate celebration.

From a human perspective on time, Bodhi spent eight or nine hours of every day being home alone, probably missing David and not having much to do. At the end of this long tract of dullness came a few minutes of joy. A human in that situation might think: "I spend 99 percent of my day just lying around and 1 percent being excited. Maybe I need to change my lifestyle." A dog would never think of it that way, because being-excited time feels much longer to an animal than lying-around time. You see, in Paradise, time is elastic. The more joyful and meaningful something is, the longer it seems to go on. In the expansiveness of that moment, whatever occurred before appears fleeting and forgettable. In the moment of reunion with David, the difference between an eight-hour separation and a five-minute one was, from Bodhi's perspective, negligible. Humans, too, are capable of experiencing time this way, and often do when we put ourselves in a situation where we don't need to tell time by the clock. When we haven't a clue what time a clock would say it is, we revert pretty quickly to a more organic relationship to time.

Animals don't dread Mondays or look forward to weekends, even though they, like us, have work time, play time, and rest time, because animals don't experience "want to" as different from "need to." They know when it's time to work because working is what they feel like doing, and when they feel like resting, that's what they do. The idea that everything an animal does has some sort of "survival value" is a projection coming from human workaholics that bears little relation to animal behavior. David Rothenberg, who wrote the book *Why Birds Sing,* made a thorough study of the matter and concluded that much of the time, birds are singing for the sheer fun of it. Often the calls they exchange aren't communicating anything of practical importance. The birds are just engaging in a jam session together. A dog who loves to chase squirrels probably has no idea what he would actually do with a squirrel if he ever caught one, and when they're not being chased by dogs, squirrels get a bang out of chasing each other. Chimpanzees turn somersaults simply because they can, and cats roll around in catmint just to get high. To be sure, animals want to survive, but to regard survival as the be-all and end-all of existence is a form of spiritual impoverishment that never afflicts them.

Animals abide in a threefold trust—trust in themselves, trust in the world, and trust in the Source. For animals it is a kind of Holy Trinity, three inseparable manifestations of a single truth. It never occurs to animals to judge themselves, or to think about themselves at all, because they experience the world as fundamentally good and themselves as inextricably connected to that source of goodness. What could possibly be wrong with them?

Human experience is an inversion of this trinity, a threefold *mistrust.* This mistrust arises whenever we disconnect from our experience in order to judge it "objectively." It doesn't really matter where you start—with negative judgments about oneself, about the world, or about God. Mistrust of one inevitably spills into the other two.

Pretty much everything in "human nature" that we ourselves judge to be bad is a consequence of our mistrust. Take greed, for example. When humans worry that, at some future date, we might not have enough of something, we take more of it than we really need in the present. Animals handle things differently. In general, a predator who has eaten his fill leaves prey animals in peace until he gets hungry again, even if he has experienced scarcity in the past.

Now I promised not to indulge in sappy nature romanticism, so let me make the other side of the case. It could be argued with some justice that humans are more successful at surviving because of the very things we do that animals don't: think abstractly, worry about the future, and work our buns off. An animal who has lived through a famine stops thinking about hunger the moment he finds something to eat. A human who has had the same experience remembers it with dismay, and comes up with a famine-prevention program. I am very glad people do this, because I like to eat. The question I want to raise here is whether it might be possible to make such beneficial *practical* arrangements without succumbing to the unhappy *spiritual* arrangements that seem to accompany them. Is threefold mistrust truly necessary to our survival as a species? Can a human partake of the paradise perspective while still holding down a job?

RESTORING TRUST

The problem of human mistrust was Jesus's central concern, and many of his teachings addressed it directly. To modern people, the word *faith* connotes intellectual belief in the unlikely. But the meaning of the Greek word that, in most editions of the gospels, is translated as "faith" is actually much closer to "trust." It refers to an orientation of the heart, rather than a conclusion of the mind. Whenever Jesus spoke of faith, he was talking about healing the mistrustful human heart.

He said,

> Don't worry about your life, about what you will eat or what you will drink, nor about your body, what you will put on. Look at the birds of the air. They neither sow nor reap nor gather into barns, yet your heavenly Father feeds them. Which of you by worrying can add one cubit to his stature? So why do you worry about clothing? Consider the lilies of the field, how they grow. They neither toil nor spin, yet I say to you that even Solomon in his glory was not decked out like one of these. Now if God so clothes the grass of the field, which is here today and thrown into the oven tomorrow, will he not much more clothe you, oh you of little trust?

Jesus's early followers understood what he was getting at—it was why they were so excited about him—but within a few generations the message had become garbled, and nobody was taking it literally any more. By the twelfth century, the bit about the lilies of the field and the birds of the air had been all but forgotten. So when a young man named Francis Bernadone took that passage to heart and turned it into a way of life, stripping off the fine clothes that had been provided by his merchant father and setting forth to wander the world with no possessions whatsoever, people at first thought that he was a lunatic. Yet they couldn't help noticing that he was a very *happy* lunatic. He seemed the happiest fellow any of them had ever met, and before long he attracted a ragtag band of followers who adopted the same blithely improvident style of life. The world now knows that young man as Saint Francis of Assisi.

Statues of St. Francis are fixtures of many gardens, for he is the patron saint of animals and the people who love them. He was renowned during his lifetime for his tenderness toward all living creatures and his ability to intuitively communicate with them. What was even more striking to people than his kindness to animals was his *respect* for them. He recognized them as individuals and treated them as equals, addressing them as "brother" and "sister." G. K. Chesterton wrote of him, "A friend of mine said that somebody was the sort of man who apologizes to the cat. St. Francis really would have apologized to the cat." He attracted such a large and boisterous entourage of critters that it was sometimes difficult for him to make himself heard when preaching to his human followers. On one such occasion, he said to a flock of chattering birds, "Little sisters, if you have now had your say, it is my turn to speak." And all the birds immediately piped down until Francis had finished his sermon.

On another occasion, Francis, while walking in the woods with other monks, noticed a massive throng of birds in the trees above him and a gathering of birds on the ground in the nearby fields. Marveling at their numbers and their beauty he said to his companions, "Wait for me here on the road. I am going to preach to our sisters and brothers, the birds." As soon as he began to preach, all the birds gathered near him, remaining motionless. Francis reminded the birds of all that God had given them to be grateful for—colorful and pretty feathers, food, their gift of singing, the domain of the air, all the rivers and springs from which they drink, the mountains, hills, rocks, the trees in which they make their homes and shelter their young. Hearing the words of Francis the birds expressed their delight by "opening their beaks, stretching out their necks, spreading their wings, then reverently bowing their heads to the ground." By their movements and their songs, the birds demonstrated to Francis their great pleasure—they rejoiced at being alive. Observing their immense joy, Francis celebrated with them, marveling at their beauty, variety, and affection. After Francis finished preaching, he gave them permission to leave, at which time they rose up into the air simultaneously and sang a most beautiful song as they flew away in different directions.

Francis lived the understanding that the natural expression of an open heart is joy, and also compassion. He once came upon a young boy who was carrying a group of live turtle doves he had caught in a snare, carrying them to market to sell. Francis, stirred by love for the innocent birds said, "Good boy, please give me those doves so that such innocent birds, symbols of pure, humble, and faithful souls, will not fall into the hands of cruel men who will kill them." The boy agreed, inspired by such compassion. Francis took the doves and made nests for all of them nearby.

Coming from a place of courtesy and deep respect, Francis was able to negotiate with animals and to mediate their conflicts with people. When a wolf was terrorizing the village of Gubbio, killing livestock and sometimes even attacking humans, the townspeople asked Francis to intervene. Francis found the wolf and, showing no fear of it whatsoever, invited him to sit down for a chat. To the astonishment of the witnesses, the wolf did so, lowering his head meekly and waiting to hear what Francis had to say. Francis then proposed a peace treaty. The wolf was to stop menacing people and killing farm animals. In exchange, the townspeople would offer him regular meals and forgive him for all his past crimes. Francis asked the wolf to signify his acceptance of this deal by shaking on it. The wolf offered his paw. From then on, he lived peaceably in the town, going door to door to ask for food and becoming so beloved that, when he finally died of old age, the people of Gubbio were sad.

It is commonly supposed that Francis was on such good terms with other creatures because he was a holy man, but I would like to suggest that it might have been more the other way around. That is, Francis's approach to human spirituality was influenced by what he learned from animals. The aspects of Jesus's teachings that other people had forgotten or misunderstood were particularly striking to Francis, because he was already on such intimate terms with the birds of the air and the grasses of the field. His respect for other living things ran so deep that he considered them worthy of emulation.

Ahead of his time, Francis saw himself as part of the ecosystem, not outside, dominating it, or master over or above it. In his "Canticle of Brother Sun" he expresses great joy, honor, and gratitude for all we have been given in this life:

> Be praised, my Lord, with all Your creatures,
> Especially Sir Brother Sun,
> By whom You give us the light of day!
> And he is beautiful and radiant with great splendor.
> Of You, Most High, he is a symbol!
>
> Be praised, my Lord, for Sister Moon and the Stars!
> In the sky, You formed them bright and lovely and fair.
>
> Be praised, my Lord for Brother Wind
> And for the Air and cloudy and clear and all Weather
> By which You give sustenance to Your creatures!
>
> Be praised, my Lord, for Sister Water,
> Who is very useful and humble and lovely and chaste!
>
> Be praised, my Lord, for Brother Fire,
> By whom You give us light at night,
> And he is beautiful and merry and mighty and strong!

Be praised my Lord, for our Sister Mother Earth,
Who sustains and governs us,
And produces fruits with colorful flowers and leaves!

The essence of Francis's approach was to restore trust by behaving in a trusting way. If you try to figure out whether the world is trustworthy before you decide to trust it, you will almost surely come to the conclusion that it is not. You can find countless examples of the various things you worry about actually coming to pass—happening to other people, if not to yourself. An intellectual overview of the world leads inevitably to mistrust, because worrying and finding facts to support one's worries are what the intellect does best.

Francis's great discovery was that you have to *act* trustingly before you can feel trust. That is, you go forth into a potentially dangerous world without preparing any defenses ahead of time. Francis and his early followers made no effort whatsoever to forestall the many unpleasant things that might happen to them. They didn't earn or carry money, didn't stockpile food, or build themselves homes, or arm themselves against outlaws. When they were hungry, they just knocked on doors and asked people for leftovers. When the weather was bad, they requested temporary shelter in a barn or shed. They learned trust by putting themselves into a precarious situation on purpose.

This is different from the popular belief that if you just have faith—i.e., "think positively"—whatever you need or want will somehow fall into your lap. God doesn't provide the lilies with Armani suits, or the birds of the air with flat-screen TVs, so there's no good reason to suppose that human faith will be productive of such amenities. Some days, when Francis and his brothers went out begging, they collected so much food that they had a surplus to give away to other beggars. Other days, they just got a stale, moldy crust of bread, or rotten vegetables, or nothing at all. Some nights they got invited into a house or loaned a blanket, but other nights they ended up shivering on the ground. In this respect, their lives were very much like those of most animals, and the trust they learned was animal trust: life is still fundamentally good even when nothing is going well on a material level. When Francis slept outdoors, Sister Moon and her attendant stars smiled down on him, and he considered himself the most fortunate man on Earth. Lady Poverty was his girlfriend, and he was head over heels in love with her.

Chesterton does a really good job of expressing how Francis's romance with poverty connected him to the Source of all life. He writes:

> It is common in a somewhat cynical sense that men have said "Blessed is he that expecteth nothing, for he shall not be disappointed." It was in a wholly happy and enthusiastic sense that St. Francis said, "Blessed is he who expecteth nothing, for he shall enjoy everything." It was by this deliberate idea of starting from zero, from the dark nothingness of his own deserts, that he did come to enjoy even earthly things as few people have enjoyed them; and they are in themselves the best working example of the idea. For there is no way in which a man can earn a star or deserve a sunset. But there is more than this involved, and more indeed than is easily to be expressed in words. It is not only true that the less a man thinks of himself, the more he thinks of his good luck and all the gifts of God. It is also true that he sees more of the things themselves when he sees more of their origin, for their origin is a part of them, and indeed the most important part of them. He sees things go forth from the divine as children going forth from a familiar and accepted home, instead of meeting them as they come out, as most of us do, upon the roads of the world.

You might be thinking that the Franciscan example is of doubtful value, since even if you were motivated to follow it, the most likely outcome nowadays would be getting thrown in jail for vagrancy. But Francis did not insist that everyone who was inspired to follow him go to such extremes. Saint Clare and his other female disciples lived in the shelter of a permanent convent. He also founded the Third Order, which encouraged people to marry and work normal jobs to support their families.

The practice of poverty doesn't have to mean giving up material security, or even material comfort. In the broadest sense, the practice of poverty is simply the practice of trust. You are practicing trust when you give up your attachment to the way you want things to be going at any given moment and surrender to the unwelcome splendor of whatever it is that's happening instead. I once got a delightful lesson in this from Francis himself.

When I visited Assisi, I was especially keen on seeing a little room where Francis sometimes used to pray and sleep. The only light comes from a small window opposite the slab of stone that Francis used as a bed. It is said that he used to lie on his back and gaze up at the stars as he prayed. I got the idea of doing this myself. I couldn't do it at night, because the room was only open to visitors during the day. But I was thrilled with the idea of lying on the exact same stone that my hero had lain on, and looking up at the exact same patch of sky. I imagined that replicating his experience would enable me to connect with him in some momentous new way.

When I got there midafternoon, the place was mobbed with tourists. The room was very small, so visitors had to queue up and wait their turn to go in. Once inside, they looked around briefly and went out again. I pressed myself against the wall—glad for once to be slight enough not to take up much space—and watched the others come and go. I figured that if I kept my vigil until it was nearly closing time, the crowds would begin to thin out and I would finally have my chance to lie on the floor unobserved. I didn't mind the wait—for I wasn't in any hurry—but the constant influx of chattering tourists annoyed me. I felt that to react with anything less than dumbstruck awe was to miss out on the significance of being admitted to this holiest of holies. I resented having to share its rarified air with these clueless, camera-toting barbarians. The longer I waited, the more irritated I became. After an hour or so, my mood had turned to full-blown misanthropy. It was then that I suddenly became aware of the presence of Saint Francis himself. He was in the room, and he was laughing his head off. He was laughing at *me!* Or rather, laughing *with* me, for as soon as I felt the laughter, I got the joke. Good one! My irritation melted into a fit of giggling. I was still laughing as I gave up on my plan and joined the herd of departing tourists.

The funny thing is that I actually got what I had been wanting: a direct encounter with Francis. It just didn't happen the way I expected it to happen. Fixated on the little ritual I had dreamed up in advance, I almost missed the very thing that the ritual was meant to accomplish. And what I got was better than what I had wanted: a private joke with Francis that still cracks me up whenever I recall it. Lying on the floor and looking up through some hole was so much *less* than what Francis had to offer me. For as he reminded me then, and continues to remind me, he is present for me whenever and wherever I want to connect with him, and no more so in his former room than anywhere else.

One of the most counterproductive of human fixations—and hardest to give up, because we so seldom notice when it's going on—is the desire to control how we are seen by others. At some level, we seem to believe that something awful will happen if other people don't see us the way we want to be seen. Though what that "something awful" might be is rarely, if ever, defined, we expend tons of energy in trying to ward it off. Francis and his followers also practiced poverty in this respect. What we would call a "self-image" was one of the items of property that they had learned to live without.

In Roberto Rossellini's film of *The Flowers of St. Francis* (based on a collection of tales that had circulated orally until they were written down during the fourteenth century), Francis gives one of his followers, Brother Ginepro, permission to go out and preach under one condition: he must begin every sermon with the words, "I talk and talk but accomplish very little." When Ginepro comes upon a village that is being terrorized by a barbarian warlord, he decides to go preach to the offenders. He strides confidently into their midst, delivers the opening line, and is met with looks of incredulity, followed by a roar of laughter. The barbarians go on to make sport of him, picking him up and tossing him around like a beach ball. Ginepro goes along cheerfully, rolling wherever he lands, and springing back up again with a silly grin. Even when they tie him to the tail of a horse and drag him around the camp on his belly, he remains remarkably uninjured. Finally they haul him before the warlord, saying that Ginepro has come into the camp to assassinate him. Since Ginepro is in immediate danger of being executed for a crime he hasn't committed, you would expect him to protest his innocence. Instead he prostrates himself at the warlord's feet, saying, "It's true—I would do all that and worse if God didn't stop me." He looks serenely happy as he says it.

Like every story associated with St. Francis, this one sounds pretty extreme. So let me offer a modern counterpart. Back when I was teaching and doing animal-rescue work in Indonesia, I got invited to a party at the American consulate. Such shindigs were not to be missed, for they featured lots of free booze and a scrumptious buffet. If you've seen the film *A Year of Living Dangerously* (in which I was an extra, but that is another story) you'll have a pretty good picture of what these parties were like. So I'm hanging out by the buffet table, champagne glass in hand, imagining myself in the Sigourney Weaver role, when this big, bluff, red-faced American sidles up to me and says, "You must be that vegetarian veterinarian I keep hearing about."

While you might read those words as a harmless statement of fact, I bristled at what was being implied. My reputation had preceded me, and that reputation was—in the speaker's eyes, and probably in the eyes of many others—for being something silly. Though the term *tree-hugger* hadn't yet been coined, "vegetarian veterinarian" meant something along the same lines. It connoted a combination of naïveté, sentimentality, and humorless fanaticism. It patronized me, and trivialized the thing I care about most passionately.

I searched my mind for the tart and witty comeback that would have rolled right off my tongue had I really been Sigourney Weaver—and drew a blank. Instead, I heard myself say cheerily, "Yes, that's me." In that instant of responding with a friendliness I didn't really feel, I looked back at the guy and really saw him. He wasn't trying to put me down. He was just expressing interest and going about it rather clumsily. As my own words—"Yes, that's me"—echoed in my mind, a delicious wave of relaxation swept over my entire body. Until then, I hadn't realized how tense I was: tense with the constant effort to get others to take me as seriously as I took myself, tense with the fear of being ridiculed and dismissed. When I allowed what I dreaded to go ahead and happen, it wasn't so awful after all. In fact, it was wonderful! Having accidentally dropped the burden of my self-importance, I didn't want to take it up again. I could travel so much lighter without it.

THE SPIRITUAL ECOSYSTEM

When God made the rule about not eating the fruit, he must have suspected that people would disobey. God had to have known that people would be curious to find out what would happen because *God* is curious to know what will happen. Where else would humans have gotten curiosity if not from our original Source?

Every species embodies some unique form of intelligence. For each aspect of the mind of the Source, there exists a species that expresses it in a heightened way. As I pointed out in the previous chapter, the particular genius of a species (what I call species-specific genius) is often a source of vulnerability for it.

Humans are really brilliant at abstract thinking. Through our thinking, we are able to apprehend aspects of the divine that other animals may never know about. We can follow the intricacies of higher mathematics and quantum physics, witness the sweep of history, and visit distant galaxies with our minds. On a practical level, our ability to detach and look at phenomena from the outside enables us to solve all sorts of problems that no other animal would know how to solve. At the same time, it enables us to create problems that no other animal could imagine having.

Even if I were silly enough to want to convince you that abstract thinking was a source of suffering that you could live very well without, you are unlikely to stop doing it any time soon. I might just as well tell squirrels to look both ways before crossing the street, or tell the Source of all life to stop creating the world. Humans are thinkers. It's what we do.

This is where ecosystems come in. The unique talent of any species can seem awkward and unwelcome if it appears in the wrong context, or in disproportion to its context. Say you're in an outdoor cafe, enjoying a breakfast of toast with strawberry jam. In that context, bees are awkward. They compete with you for a taste of the jam, and you're nervous that you might swallow one by accident, or get stung. You would like to be rid of them. On the other hand, if there were no bees, there would be no strawberries to put in the jam. In the context of a berry farm, you totally approve of bees.

Often we have no idea what an awkward species is for until we manage to get rid of it. When ranchers wanted to kill off the wolves in and around Yellowstone National Park because they were preying on livestock, they encountered little opposition. According to the Endangered Species Act, wolves were "nonessential." But a few years after the wolves were eliminated, the forests started to thin out. Elks like to feed on young trees and, no longer threatened by wolves, their population was soaring. None of the young trees were living long enough to replace the older trees as they died off. The thinning of the forest meant a loss of habitat for many other species, who started to die off too. So the Park Service introduced coyotes to bring the elk population down. Trouble was, coyotes found it easier to catch foxes than to catch elk, so pretty soon the foxes started dying out. The park became overrun with coyotes and the elk went on munching everything in sight. The only thing for it to do was to bring back the wolves. They were reintroduced in 1995, and since then the park has gradually been restored to balance. Wolves might be awkward if you are a cattle rancher, but they are nevertheless indispensable.

Every creature has a purpose that you might not be able to see if you are looking at that creature in isolation. As a biological fact, this is probably already familiar to you, so I won't belabor it. Instead I want to draw your attention to its spiritual correlative. Paradise is a spiritual ecosystem in which every species has some essential role to play. The problem with people is not that there is anything wrong with human nature in and of itself. The problem is that people are becoming to the spiritual ecosystem what the elk became to Yellowstone after the wolves were subtracted. Our spiritual ecosystem is out of whack because there's too much human nature in it and not enough of other forms of nature.

At an earlier stage in human history, the cause of wars between humans was, for the most part, disputes over territory or resources—the same thing animals are fighting about when they fight. As people have become more "civilized"—that is, more isolated from other species in our day-to-day lives—the cause of armed conflict has shifted more and more toward ideology. We kill each other over thoughts. Abstract thinking, which has great survival value if you're trying to navigate an ocean or prevent an outbreak of polio, has become one of our greatest survival threats. Abstraction isn't an evil in itself, but it runs amok when it's not balanced by other perspectives on the world. It is our fellow creatures who provide those perspectives.

For many of us, it is becoming more and more feasible to live in an entirely manmade world, to rush from one manmade container to another such container, by means of yet another container, without ever encountering a nonhuman life form. Nothing could be more detrimental to our emotional and spiritual health. As a species, we need to live in close and regular contact with creatures who are different from us, especially animals. This is as true for each of us as individuals as it is for humanity as a whole.

It can be as simple as this: you are sitting alone, engaging in unhappy introspection, finding fault with yourself and your life. The more you think, the more dejected you feel. While you are lost in such discouraging abstractions, your dog comes over to lie at your feet and lick your toes. You have introspected your way into a belief that you are pretty much worthless and here is your dog, paying you this homage. Your dog can't conceive of ever liking or admiring anyone more. To your dog, you are the apex of human perfection. Your dog, at that moment, is expressing God's view of the matter. To do so is a dog's role in the spiritual ecosystem.

Or say you are taking out the garbage before leaving for work on a Monday morning. You're in a hurry and your thoughts are one long and fretful to-do list. You don't have time to stop and listen to a bird, but a bird is insisting that you listen, all but grabbing you by the lapels with the sweetness of its song. The singing makes you lose your place on the to-do list. It washes over you like a refreshing shower and makes you smile. To make you smile on a Monday morning is a tough job, but somebody's got to do it.

You might think that you don't know how to expand the present moment until it's big enough to bask in. That's okay. You don't need to know. The bird knows how and does it for you. A dog knows how and is delighted to oblige. Even a fly crawling across your kitchen table knows how. All you need to do is to give these creatures an opening. They're at your service.

The meditation with which I began this chapter is based on an experience I had as a small child. I got it from a robin. My robin friend was singing, and his song was making me really happy. The happiness grew and grew until it sort of exploded, and the rest of the world seemed to be exploding with it—exploding in a happy way—right before my eyes. Back then, I didn't know anything about atoms or molecules or subatomic particles, nor had I studied any of the wisdom traditions. The name I gave to what I was seeing was "bubbles." The inside of me felt like it was made of bubbles, and everything on the outside looked like it was made of bubbles. The edges of things became less clearly defined—the robin, the trees, my own arm—no separation between the ending of one and the beginning of the other. Feeling on the inside the way things looked on the outside let me know that I was part of everything else and everything else was part of me. This knowledge seemed to be coming directly from the robin's singing. I felt he was telling it to me in so many chirps.

All these years later, the song of a robin still affects me that way. My spirit takes wing and circles a few laps around Paradise.

Chapter 5

YOU DON'T HAVE TO
FIGURE EVERYTHING OUT

Every animal knows more than you do.

—NATIVE AMERICAN PROVERB

A cat is a puzzle for which there is no solution.

—HAZEL NICHOLSON

Whoever undertakes to set himself up as a judge of truth and knowledge is ship-wrecked by the laughter of the gods.

—ALBERT EINSTEIN

When I was a kid, I'd pester my dad incessantly with questions. I probably drove him nuts because every answer led to another question, and like most kids I would not be put off. He was very patient. He would often answer, "I don't know. What do you think?" or "People just don't know. Only God knows."

God came into it frequently, for children don't especially distinguish between scientific and metaphysical questions. I wanted to know where we all came from and why we were here. Why was there something and not nothing? A child doesn't regard that question as essentially different from "What makes the stove get hot?" Children are eager to know how the world works at every level, for they have faith that it does work at every level. I was positive that the most exciting things were happening at the edges of the known, and that my questions had the power to carry me to that thrilling place.

It was Socrates who said, "The unexamined life is not worth living." Socrates also said, "The only true wisdom is in knowing that you know nothing." That is the essential paradox of the human drive to question: it is an itch that just gets itchier when you scratch it. The more you learn, the more you know that you *don't* know. Every clue just seems to lead you deeper into mystery. Seeking a synthesis embracing both rational understanding and the mystical experience of unity, the Nobel Prize-winning physicist Erwin Schrodinger once said, "The scientific picture of the world around me is very deficient. It gives me a lot of factual information, puts all our experience in a magnificently consistent order, but it is ghastly silent about all and sundry that is really dear to our heart, that really matters to us."

Over the centuries, our collective quest for knowledge has led to impressive discoveries. Yet every answer seems to open on to a new and more difficult question. Every answer implies a new "but *why?*" Neuroscience can tell us a great deal about the activity of the brain, but can't explain what consciousness is, where it is located, or where it comes from. Rudolph Tanzi, PhD, is the Joseph P. and Rose F. Kennedy Professor of Neurology at Harvard University and director of the Genetics and Aging Research Unit at Massachusetts General Hospital. In his new book, *Super Brain,* coauthored with Deepak Chopra, MD, he says, "old beliefs that need to go" include the long-standing dogma that says "the brain creates consciousness. In reality, it's the other way around." The book also assures us that "memory remains elusive. It leaves no physical traces in the brain cells, and no one really knows how our memories are stored." Science does not have an answer to what makes the human heart begin beating. Medical science has extended human life expectancy, but can't tell us why (or even *if*) life must inevitably end in death. In physics, the principle that nothing can travel faster than the speed of light seems to hold up, yet nobody knows for sure why this speed limit is absolute, or even whether it is absolute. In the Big Bang Theory, most astronomers find a satisfactory explanation of how the universe as we know it began, but the theory doesn't tell us what happened before the Big Bang (therefore it remains only a theory) or predict how or when or whether the universe will end. Menas Kafatos, physicist and professor of interdisciplinary science at George Mason University, reminds us in his book, *The Non-Local Universe,* that at this time there is no universally held view of the actual character of physical reality in biology or physics. The physical universe on the most basic level remains what it has always been— a riddle.

To be sure, these are the most ancient and perplexing of human questions. Yet even some questions that don't sound all that difficult remain unanswered. Veterinary science has so far been unable to explain the mechanics of a cat's purr, or why small cats purr but big cats like lions and tigers do not. We don't know why wolves howl at the moon, or how birds learn complex migratory routes after just one flight. So far, we've managed to identify 1.4 million species living on Earth. What we don't know is how many unidentified species remain. Estimates range from under one million to over a hundred million. And sadly, sometimes we have learned how a species worked perfectly in the web of life only after it became extinct and we saw the imbalance created.

If you are like most people, the notion that millions of species remain to be discovered probably pleases you, for there is something in the human psyche that delights in exploration and discovery, and would be dismayed to think there was nothing new left to find. Imagine some distant, hypothetical future when all that the universe contained had been catalogued, classified, and explained, a time when human learning had answered every question and eradicated every mystery. No matter how much you crave answers, you probably wouldn't want to live in such a time. (Not that there is any danger of its ever really arriving.) What would people do with themselves? With every source of curiosity extinguished, would residents of this imaginary world even be recognizable as humans?

What excites us is potential, the feeling of being on the verge of a discovery that is almost within reach yet not quite yet within our grasp. If Dad can answer our first question, we immediately come up with a harder one, for the questions that stump Dad are where our wonder lies. What Dad—or science—can't answer is known only to the Source of all, and it is toward that Source that all our questions are ultimately leading. Human inquisitiveness is our built-in Source-seeking device, our spiritual homing instinct.

COMPLAINTS TO THE MANAGEMENT

For small children, curiosity is an unmixed delight. But as we get older, the leading edge of our curiosity begins to feel a bit, well, *edgy*.

When asked by a five-year-old, "Why are we here?" is a juicy and cheerful question that the child expects will lead to a juicy and cheerful answer. Coming from a grown-up, the same question often sounds more like a complaint to the management. There's a subtext that runs, "I'm not entirely liking it here, so whoever created this setup and put me in it had better have a damn good reason!"

That plaintive edge to our questioning begins to creep in as a result of another of our "God-given" human attributes: our imagination. We can picture the world being different than it actually is, and not only different, but better. And once we start to picture it better, we wonder why it was not created the way we are picturing it. A little kid who asks, "Why does it rain?" is expressing wonderment over a delightful and surprising phenomenon: how does it work, exactly? As we get older, our question is more likely to be, "Why does it always rain on my parade?" We conceive of ideals like fairness, generosity, and unconditional love, and feel both baffled and despondent when the actual world doesn't match up with these ideals. Because ideals are an expression of our spiritual nature, we can't understand why a God-created world does not seem to operate in accordance with them. Why does God permit people to be eaten alive by cancer, or to perish in natural disasters, or to be born to parents who neglect and abuse them? Furthermore, why put ideals in our minds if they're only going to lead to disappointment? Why are we capable of imagining a better world than the one we've been given to live in? For that matter, how do we even know that there *is* a God?

Such questions don't merely concern suffering: they are a form of suffering in themselves, an additional layer of suffering *about* suffering. We do this suffering about suffering that isn't even our own. In fact, our spiritual discomfort is at its worst when we witness the suffering of others and are unable to do anything to help. We can't stand it when life is cruel or unfair for anyone. We hold it against God, and then suffer all the more from that spiritual estrangement.

Animals don't have this difficulty. Animals suffer both emotionally and physically, but they don't suffer metaphysically. That is, they don't suffer *about* suffering, don't get thrown into spiritual confusion by it, or fall out of connection with the divine because of it. They don't try to figure out why suffering is happening, or imagine a world in which something different or better might be happening. Maybe we would suffer less if we could learn to emulate the animals in this respect, learn to just take life as it comes without trying so hard to understand the why of it. But that's a bit like saying that deer would suffer less if they didn't try to dart across busy highways, or that dogs would suffer less if they didn't become emotionally attached to people who neglect them. True enough, but not especially helpful. Every living creature has in her very nature something that renders her vulnerable to getting hurt in a particular way. And the quality that renders her vulnerable is often her best quality, her particular genius as a species.

So it is with humans. We suffer estrangement from the divine as a side effect of the best gifts our Source has given us, the very qualities that are our spiritual "homing instinct": our inquisitiveness and our imagination. Because we can imagine alternatives to the natural way of things, we are the only species that ever hunts purely for sport (a human behavior that predator animals regard as truly bizarre). But we are also the only carnivorous creatures who can imagine becoming vegetarian, and can actually decide to do so. Even if it were possible, getting rid of our yearning for answers is not the remedy for our spiritual discomfort.

In the Book of Job, the Bible tackles this problem head-on. At the start of the story, Job is a prosperous farmer. He owns 500 donkeys, 500 oxen, 7,000 sheep, and 3,000 camels. He is happy, healthy, and the proud father of ten children. He is also exceptionally religious, and re-garded by everyone (including himself) as a good and righteous man.

Then his luck begins to change. All of his animals are stolen, except for the camels, who perish when a mysterious fire falls from the sky. All of his children are killed when a windstorm destroys the house of his firstborn. Job manages to take these calamities in stride, saying, "The Lord has given and the Lord has taken away. Blessed be the name of the Lord." But that's not the end of his misfortunes. He comes down with a terrible illness, his entire body covered in boils so painful that he can't put on clothes. This, too, he bears with remarkably good grace.

What pushes Job to the edge is not his afflictions themselves, but the well-meaning ministrations of the friends who come to console him. As his friends see it, Job's misfortunes must be his own fault. God must be punishing him. Job insists that this cannot be the case, for he has done nothing wrong. His friends agree that he has committed no wrong that is apparent to them, then exhort him to search his conscience for a wrong so secret and subtle that it is apparent only to God. Job thinks about it some more and comes back with the same answer: there is nothing on his conscience that would justify such an extreme chastisement. The conversation goes on for many repetitive pages, running around and around in the same unproductive circles because Job's friends are unable to conceive of the problem in any other way. They are starting from the premise that the world is based on God's laws, that these laws are just, and that everything God does is some kind of law enforcement. If something occurs that appears to be unjust, the fault must lie in human interpretation. What the friends refuse to admit into their awareness is the possibility that some misfortunes are inexplicable, for that would blow apart their whole concept of what God is and how the world operates. Job is unable to refute their view with an alternative explanation. He has absolutely no idea why so much suffering has befallen him. All he knows for sure is that it can't possibly be a punishment.

After many wearisome pages of this debate, God finally shows up, appearing "on a whirlwind." He basically takes Job's side, agreeing that Job has done nothing wrong and rebuking the friends for insisting that Job is being punished. Then he goes on to have a private word (quite a few words, actually) with Job himself. In painstaking detail, God boasts of the many things he has created. He starts with the elements—wind, water, fire, and so forth—describing how he commands the weather, over which humans are powerless. Then he moves on to the animals. As a farmer, Job had owned and been able to control a variety of domesticated species. God draws his attention to their undomesticated counterparts—the mountain goat, the wild ox, and wild ass—pointing out how these animals cannot be constrained to serve human needs. He goes on to describe the unique abilities and behaviors of other wild species, pointing out how different they are from the abilities and behaviors of humans.

> The wings of the ostrich wave proudly,
> but are they the pinions and plumage of love?
> For she leaves her eggs to the earth,
> and lets them be warmed on the ground,
> forgetting that a foot may crush them,
> and that the wild beast may trample them.
> She deals cruelly with her young, as
> if they were not hers;
> though her labor be in vain, yet
> she has no fear;
> because God has made her forget wisdom,
> and given her no share in understanding.
> When she rouses herself to flee,
> she laughs at the horse and his rider.

"Do you give the horse his might?" God continues. "Is it by your wisdom that the hawk soars?" he demands. "Is it at your command that the eagle mounts up and makes his nest on high?"

By now Job is beginning to get the drift. "Behold, I am of small account," he replies. "What shall I answer thee? I lay my hand upon my mouth."

But God is just getting warmed up. He goes on to boast of having created the Behemoth, an enormous land animal, and Leviathan, a fearsome sea monster. Scholars debate whether these names refer to actual animals (a hippopotamus, perhaps, and a whale) or mythological ones. Either way, what God is saying in these passages holds true: that humans share the Earth with creatures that startle and sometimes terrify us in their size, their power, and their sheer foreignness to our physical and psychological experience. These creatures are not only beyond human control, but beyond human imagination. What has sprung from the mind of the Source would never have sprung from the mind of Job.

Thirty-four verses of description later in Leviathan, Job finally grasps the relationship between God's answer and his own question. "I know that thou canst do all things and that no purpose of thine can be thwarted," he says. "Therefore I have uttered what I did not understand, things too wonderful for me, which I did not know. I have heard of thee by the hearing of the ear, but now my eyes see thee."

At this point, you might be asking yourself, "What am I missing?" What do ostriches, mountain goats, and whales have to do with the problem of suffering?

God isn't saying that Job is mistaken in his human notions of right and wrong, or in his belief that he did nothing to deserve his affliction. He is saying rather that these correct beliefs are just a small part of a much bigger picture—a picture that Job hasn't been able to see because he expects everything he encounters to conform to his own concepts, his own notion of the divine order. Out of unbridled creative exuberance, the Source brings into existence every possibility that comes to mind. Many of these possibilities are startling to human sensibilities. Some scare us, and a few are downright offensive to us. The sheer weirdness of some of the creatures that coinhabit our world demonstrates the limits of our understanding. Divine mind has imagined things that we ourselves would never have imagined in a million years.

William Blake expresses a very similar idea in his poem "The Tiger":

TIGER, tiger, burning bright
In the forests of the night,

What immortal hand or eye
Could frame thy fearful symmetry?

In what distant deeps or skies
Burnt the fire of thine eyes?
On what wings dare he aspire?
What the hand dare seize the fire?

And what shoulder and what art
Could twist the sinews of thy heart?
And when thy heart began to beat,
What dread hand and what dread feet?

What the hammer? what the chain?
In what furnace was thy brain?
What the anvil? What dread grasp
Dare its deadly terrors clasp?

When the stars threw down their spears,
And water'd heaven with their tears,
Did He smile His work to see?
Did He who made the lamb make thee?

In *Songs of Innocence and of Experience,* the tiger poem is paired with one about a lamb. It begins:

Little Lamb, who made thee?
Dost thou know who made thee?
Gave thee life, and bid thee feed
By the stream and o'er the mead;
Gave thee clothing of delight,
Softest clothing, woolly, bright;
Gave thee such a tender voice,
Making all the vales rejoice?

Little Lamb, who made thee?
Dost thou know who made thee?

It is by juxtaposing these two contrasting poems—one so fierce, the other so tender—that Blake expresses the range of divine creativity and the puzzle it presents to the human mind.

Animal Cultures and Human Prejudices

For many people, a sense of wonderment at the inscrutable otherness of creation comes most readily from beholding nature's really big special effects: Niagara Falls, the Grand Canyon, a towering redwood tree, or a meteor shower. In such phenomena we recognize something awesome happening to which human thoughts, emotions, and values are entirely irrelevant. But it is in animals that we find a more familiar, and in some ways more accessible, bridge between humanness and otherness, for animals have thoughts, emotions, and values of their own. Each species is a culture unto itself. Each one has a unique perspective on the world, and a set of customs arising from that perspective. Each has its own notion of what we might call virtue, and its own taboos. Each has a unique set of interests, aspirations, and talents. Some of these cultures couldn't be more different than our own, yet if we study them closely, they are intelligible to us as cultures. To look at an animal's culture from that animal's own point of view is to glimpse some aspect of divine mind that is foreign to the human mind, yet not entirely incomprehensible to it.

Let's start with a foreign culture we can watch from our own backyards: that of the common squirrel. What strikes us immediately is how carefree squirrels appear to be. When they're not finding food and burying it, the adults behave like children. They play tag with each other, leap from tree to tree, and engage in circus acrobatics for the sheer fun of it. No matter how high they climb or how far they leap, they seem oblivious to danger. It is as if they believe themselves to be indestructible. A squirrel can fall from a height of one hundred feet without being injured, its tail acting as a parachute. Imagine what your life would be like if falling weren't dangerous to you. Think of the fun you could have. Squirrels take a lot of risks, attempting leaps that are beyond their abilities. They have no fear of risk because failure so rarely results in harm. The lack of fear probably contributes to the lack of injury—they are completely relaxed when they fall—and the lack of injury contributes to the relaxation. Squirrel play is a sort of happy feedback loop that leads to ever more daring exploits.

Squirrels enjoy a longer infancy than most other rodents. Born when they are only an inch long and completely hairless, they spend an average of four months in the nest before they are weaned. (Baby mice, by contrast, are weaned after two or three weeks.) They experience a prolonged period of safety and maternal love before venturing out into the world. This, too, contributes to their culture of exuberance. It is as if, through the squirrel, our Source is indulging in an endless happy childhood.

From a human perspective, squirrels are careless as well as carefree. Getting run over by cars is the leading cause of premature squirrel fatalities. This is a good example of what I meant when I said that the particular genius of a species (their species-specific genius) is also a source of vulnerability for it. What makes life worth living for a squirrel is often what gets it killed. A cautious squirrel—one who could learn to wait at the corner for the light to turn green—would not be a squirrel at all. If you ponder that a while, perhaps you will begin to see the answer to Job in it.

I began with the squirrel because it is at once familiar and charming. Now let's consider another member of the rodent family: the bat. From our human perspective, why Source created this creature is not immediately obvious. Many people find bats creepy. All an artist needs to do to put across the idea that a house is haunted is to draw bats flying around it.

Contrary to popular belief, bats are not blind. Many of them are able to see parts of the light spectrum that are invisible to humans. In addition to having good eyesight, they possess a sense of echolocation so finely tuned that they can detect objects as thin as a single human hair. (Getting tangled in your hair is the very last thing a bat would ever do.) If you're plagued by flying insect pests, a bat would be really handy to have around. A single bat can eat as many as six hundred bugs in an hour, which is the equivalent of a human consuming twenty pizzas in one sitting. An even more crucial bat contribution to the ecosystem is the spreading of seeds. Some seeds will not germinate unless they have passed through a bat's digestive tract. Roughly 95 percent of new growth in the tropical rain forest is the result of seed dispersal by bats.

An instinctive—or perhaps superstitious—aversion to creatures like bats, snakes, cockroaches, and other creepy crawlers is just one of the challenges we face when attempting to appreciate the unique aspect of the divine that each species expresses. In trying to understand animal cultures, we humans tend to make the same mistake that Job's friends made in trying to understand God: we assume that human values are the measure of everything.

The natural sciences have traditionally proceeded from a premise that has its roots in medieval theology. The premise is that nature is a hierarchy, a sort of ladder of evolutionary achievement with one-celled organisms on the bottom rung and human beings at the top. Even scientists who profess to be atheists seem to take it on faith that humanity is the pinnacle of Creation and enjoys dominion over all other creatures. This assumption can be our blind spot on a scientific level as well as on a spiritual one.

Characteristics such as a large and complex brain, the use of tools, linguistic sophistication, and the ability to transmit knowledge through culture are considered the hallmarks of species superiority, because they happen to be human characteristics. For humans to come out the winners of a competition in which we have made the rules is hardly surprising. But the more we learn about other creatures, the more we discover that nature isn't following the human rule-book.

The hierarchical assumption would lead us to expect the animals who are most like us—the large primates—to come out on top of other animals in the superiority rankings. The fact that larger primates can be taught to use tools, albeit in a clumsy and primitive way, supports both our belief in the hierarchy and in the qualitative superiority of our own intelligence. That is, it did until someone noticed that crows could use tools, and were a lot better at it than apes.

Yes, *crows*. In the wild, New Caledonian crows use sticks to dig insects out of logs. Rather than rely on whatever sticks might be lying around, they select twigs that have the needed length and circumference, strip them of leaves and trim them if necessary. In a series of experiments performed in captivity, New Caledonian crows quickly figured out how to fashion tools in different shapes and out of different materials than those used in the wild. One experiment challenged the crows with a piece of meat that could only be retrieved by fishing for it with a hook. Offered a selection of both straight and hooked lengths of fencing wire, they chose the hooked ones. If only straight wire was available, the crows bent it themselves. Even more remarkably, they engaged in what is called *metatool use*—that is, using one tool to make or obtain another. Until recently, it was believed that metatool use was unique to humans. But the crows, who obviously hadn't gotten the memo on human uniqueness, employed a variety of other objects to bend the straight wires into hooks. They also used wires that were within reach to retrieve more desirable wires that were out of reach.

It turns out that humans don't hold the patent on linguistic sophistication, either. The study of language in animals is complicated by some differences of opinion over how language should be defined. Many species make sounds or gestures that are meaningful to others of their species, but sounds and gestures are not necessarily words. A chimpanzee may learn that he will be rewarded with a piece of candy if he makes the signs for "want" and "candy," but it can be argued that what the chimp has learned is merely a stimulus-response pattern. In language as linguists define it, words used in one context can be recombined to describe new phenomena and experiences. Grammar and syntax can be used to alter or refine the meaning of words. (Example: "Car hits man." vs. "Man hits car.")

When taught to hand-sign, the larger primates can pick up and use a rudimentary vocabulary of human words, but they haven't been able to progress beyond what, in human terms, is baby talk. Nor, as far as we can tell, do primates bother to learn a language unless bribed to do so by humans. Treats seem to motivate them more than any yearning for self-expression. Once again, it appeared that the race between humans and our nearest runner-up in the intelligence sweepstakes wasn't even close. Or so we thought until someone figured out what prairie dogs have been saying to each other all these years.

Prairie dogs are cute little rodents with simple little brains. The list of predators who like to feed on them is a mile long, and as if that weren't bad enough, gun-crazy humanoids like to use them for target practice. You might expect animals in that predicament to be constantly on the run, but prairie dogs are homebodies. Colonies of them have lived in the same burrows for hundreds of years. As a result, they are on intimate terms with their predators, who know exactly where to find them. The prairie dogs are able to survive because they communicate with each other in sentences. Instead of just making sounds of generalized alarm when a threat is approaching, the first prairie dog to spot it tells the others what kind of threat it is, where it's coming from, how far away it is, and how fast it is approaching. When the threat is a human, they describe the person's size, what color clothes the person is wearing, and whether the person is carrying a gun.

The scientist who first learned to decipher their language, Dr. Con Slobodchikoff, discovered that different colonies use different dialects, which suggests that the language is being transmitted culturally (that is, by the adults teaching the young) rather than genetically. In one experiment, he demonstrated that prairie dogs could adapt existing words to describe new phenomena. He constructed plywood silhouettes in the shape of predator animals and used a pulley to position them near the colony. The prairie dogs responded to each silhouette with a different alarm call, which suggests that they were saying more than "unidentified threatening object." The call that referred to the plywood coyote was a variant on the sound made to announce real coyotes. Grammatically and syntactically, this is the most sophisticated animal language ever to be deciphered by humans. And the prairie dogs didn't learn it from people. They made it up themselves.

What's great about the persistent effort to find scientific grounds for human superiority is that it keeps failing in such interesting ways.

To be sure, there are human abilities that other animals lack, but the more we learn about animals, the more abilities we discover that humans lack. Obviously if animals were included in the Olympics, humans wouldn't take home many gold medals. We can't run as fast as a cheetah, swim as well as a fish, or lift as much weight as an elephant. What is more surprising is that if we define intelligence as the ability to solve survival problems creatively, we are not the clear winners either. (To give you just one rather silly example: so far, the human effort to design a raccoon-proof garbage receptacle has failed, resulting only in smarter raccoons.) Every species embodies a solution to some environmental challenge, and some of these solutions are breathtaking in their elegance.

There are as many forms of genius in the world as there are species. If we drop our preoccupation with human superiority, we can recognize in these many forms of genius the mind of the Source at play.

ANIMAL MORALITY AND HUMAN VALUES

In the Book of Job, God's description of the ostrich opens with a question: "The wings of the ostrich wave proudly, but are they the pinions and plumage of love?" God doesn't answer the question, but offers evidence that appears damning, for the female ostrich leaves her eggs where they are in danger of being trampled and "deals cruelly with her young." From a human perspective, the ostrich appears to be a lousy mother.

Ostriches lay their eggs in communal nests. Once all the eggs are present, the dominant female sorts through them, discarding those that have been laid by the weakest females. She and all the other ostriches take turns protecting the remaining eggs. It is true that female ostriches have little to do with their young once the eggs have hatched. That is because, in ostrich culture, child-rearing is primarily the responsibility of the males. In an inner contact with me, an ostrich explained it like this:

Our nests attract many predators, for we gather our eggs together. Because humans also seek our eggs, I will explain that every egg is known to our highest order female. She rules the nest and knows which eggs will produce the strongest young, those having the best chance to survive. She will sacrifice the weaker eggs to save the strong. We understand nature's laws. We trust Earth Spirit and Sky Spirit to help guide the ones who remain with us.

That is how the matter of proper maternal behavior looks from an ostrich's own point of view. When you read the passage from Job with this in mind, you can see that God's question was not what it might first have appeared. The point is not that ostriches do not love, but that love may express itself in ways that are unfathomable to the human mind. God is saying that Job is having trouble understanding God in the same way that people may misunderstand the ostrich: by assuming that the entire universe should be judged by human moral values.

Back in the day when the belief in human superiority was at its most robust, people took it for granted that a conscience—a sense of right and wrong—was what distinguished humans from all other species. The argument was somewhat solipsistic in that the definition of "right" was essentially "what humans do that animals don't." Humans, for instance, have sexual inhibitions whereas the animals with which humans were most familiar appeared to mate on very short acquaintance. Now we know that this assumption about animal sexuality was based mainly on prejudice and ignorance, for animal cultures offer an astonishing variety of reproductive customs and mores. While their sexual taboos might be quite different from ours, most animal cultures have them. Still, it remains true to this day that one of the worst adjectives you can apply to a human being is "bestial."

Since Darwin, attitudes have begun to shift in the opposite direction, as many people look to animalistic human behavior to explain human psychology and inform human moral behavior. Some will say that promiscuous impulses on the part of the human male are natural (read: okay to indulge) because they have survival value. The male's job is to impregnate as many females as possible to ensure that the human species doesn't go extinct. This way of thinking is only slightly less misinformed than the belief in human moral superiority. It is still trying to establish a single standard of moral judgment for all species. It is my understanding from an intuitive relationship with animals that it is complete folly to try to figure out what is right or wrong for humans by observing what other animals are doing. Observe any animal and you will quickly figure out that a hawk does not try to hunt like an eagle. The wolf does not try to be a lion.

The imagination of the Source of all life is inexhaustible. Any behavior we can conceive of—and perhaps many that we could never have conceived of—occurs in some species or another. Even if we were to learn what to do by emulating animals, which animal should it be? Squirrels' nests are hastily put together and not built to last. Should a nest become infested with fleas or discovered by predators, the squirrels will abandon it without regret and make a new one. Since squirrels are conspicuously happy, we might conclude that humans could be equally happy if we would stop investing in real estate. But prairie dogs, who are the squirrels' nearest biological relatives, treat their underground dwellings like ancestral domains, passing them from generation to generation for hundreds of years. No matter how hassled they are by predators, prairie dogs will not abandon their homes. Both behaviors work. It is impossible to conclude that nature endorses or condemns the principle of home ownership.

The issue of predation is particularly troubling to humans because it feels to us, on an emotional level, like something bad. The word that springs most readily to our minds is "cruel." The fact that, in order to survive, every species has to eat some other species (a plant or plant product, if not an insect or an animal), and that hardly anything can eat without causing a death, feels inconsistent with love. How can I insist that love is the basic building block of life—that the word "life" is synonymous with "love"—in a world where the strong live by devouring the weak? How could a loving, divine mind have set it up that way? Here again, some people overreact in the opposite direction. If nature is cruel, human cruelty must be natural. When nature documentaries depict animals killing and eating their prey, some people look on in fascination, deriving a vicarious thrill. What is especially annoying is how these documentaries leave out any other aspect of an animal's culture. What is missing from both of the previous assumptions is the animal's own point of view.

I have spent years both observing animals in the wild, and reflecting on my intuitive understanding regarding predation. Predator/prey relations are a big deal to animals. Human misconceptions about it cause us a lot of spiritual difficulties that they, the animals, could clear up if we would only pay more attention to what is really involved in what we call "the circle of life." We humans have much to learn about "relationship" in nature. There is a sacred connection that exists between predator and prey animals. The distinction between taking and receiving is crucially important, and is stressed by predator and prey animals alike. Both understand the life of the prey to be a gift to the predator. What I have received from animals on the matter is the following:

The beings, plants, fruits, grasses all have life and purpose. The beings who eat the flesh of others have meaning and purpose as do the ones they eat—and all have desire to live. There is nothing in the whole of nature that is considered "not alive" or without purpose. Therefore, it is important to understand that all beings serve other beings.

Like life, all food is a gift. We share our bodies as food for the greater good of all; this is the natural process of life and death in the wild. We are not so afraid of death. We are much more concerned about life, living, and surviving every day. We gather only what we need to survive and do not waste. The word kindness resonates, to help describe the bigger meaning of prey/predator. Why? Because the Source feeds all, and this means giving, not taking. *Giving, allowing,* and *receiving* are the words to describe prey/predator. Yes, those words are correct. Nature offers. There is not taking. The Source of all and nature give generously, so that all may prosper. We give of ourselves (sometimes this involves giving up our life) and all receive.

The cycle of life and death is nature's law, which is Source law. There is no life without death, and death is not the end of life: all life in nature understands this. In death, we become another part of the cycle. When we are caught as prey, our life force, our energy, and body become part of the one who now lives because of us. Nature has provided our body as life for another, and we are part of nature's law, so as much as we fight for life, we are part of nature's law, and love. We trust the way of nature. Our earthly body and energy (never our soul), becomes part of the being who feeds on our body.

This is sacred, do you understand? In the wild, predator has great respect and gratitude for prey. This is a powerful and intimate bond, predator/prey. Yes, one lives and one meets death, but there is no good/bad.

The one who becomes prey, who becomes life for another, finds that death comes quickly. It is like this for two reasons. One is the word used before—*kindness*—for struggle is not good for prey or predator energetically. Two, the body as fresh and alive as possible is most healthy. The prey, even if wounded or old, has a life that has been free, experienced the joy of living and love in their own culture. This has created vitality and health in the energy and body of the prey, which then adds health and vibrant energy to the body of the predator. Remember, a predator may later become prey for another. This is very important.

Misunderstanding of predator/prey relationships has led to human mistreatment of the animals we eat for food.

Human's prey animals are not allowed to live as nature intended. A free, purposeful, joyous life is denied them. Sorrow and fear become their entire story. Their life energy is drained. They become sick. They are left to experience only communal fear, dread of the fate before them. Physical and emotional suffering is great and remains imprinted in the energy and body parts of these beings. The history of the life of the animal then becomes part of the one who eats this being. Remember, what you do to nature you do to self. It is known that the beings bred and raised as (what is the word?) prisoners in cages—if you are inflicting cruelty and suffering on the being you eat, what manifests in the body of that prisoner in a cage becomes part of your body, your energy, when you eat. This cannot be otherwise. Much needs to be corrected in human prey/predator ways, for all are suffering greatly, the humans also.

What is most striking about the animals and the predation question is that they don't question the Source's wisdom and love. Why one being must die so another can live is a mystery that they cannot explain, yet it doesn't trouble them. Both predator and prey find their relationship beautiful, and sacred. Surrendering to the cycle endows their lives with meaning and brings them a sense of peace: a peace that arises at the point where what is known dissolves into what cannot be known.

THE CLOUD OF UNKNOWING

Albert Einstein once wrote, "Curiosity has its own reason for existing." Since his curiosity led to important discoveries, you might expect him to say that curiosity exists so that we can find things out. But that is not where Einstein was going with the topic. His next sentence reads: "One cannot help but be in awe when he contemplates the mysteries of eternity, of life, of the marvelous structure of reality."

The purpose of curiosity is to carry us to the brink of mystery. The benefit of curiosity is that it enables us to experience awe. "It is enough if one tries merely to comprehend a little of this mystery every day," Einstein said. "Never lose a holy curiosity."

This holy curiosity keeps us humble. Russell Targ begins his book, *The Reality of ESP*, with a quote from Carl Jung, "I shall not commit the fashionable stupidity of regarding everything I cannot explain as a fraud." Our egos have a tendency to seduce and delude us into thinking we can solve all the mysteries of life. When we think we know the answer for sure, we close to new possibilities, new discoveries waiting to be found.

Saint Thomas Aquinas, who lived in the thirteenth century, was one of the smartest men of his time. His best known work, *Summa Theologica,* sets forth the whole of Christian doctrine and gamely takes on such difficult riddles as "How can we know for sure that there is a God?" and "What is the purpose of human life?" The word "Summa" means all. In contemporary terms, his title might be translated, "Everything You've Ever Wanted to Know about God." In other words, Thomas was a bit of a know-it-all. He never met a question he didn't believe he could answer.

During the last year of his life, Thomas was celebrating Mass when, according to his early biographers, Christ appeared to him, praised him for having lived such a meritorious life, and asked what he would like to have in return. Thomas is said to have replied, "Only you, Lord." Nobody knows what happened next, because Thomas never spoke or wrote of it. In fact, he never wrote another word. When his secretary begged him to get back to work on his books, Thomas replied, "I cannot, because all that I have written seems like straw to me."

There it is again: the central paradox of our drive to question. Sometimes we really do find answers, and we are thrilled by our ability to discover and understand them. But it is when we come to the limits of our understanding that we glimpse the divine. It is as if the very purpose of our intelligence is to stretch until it reaches its limit and snaps. The Danish theologian Soren Kierkegaard wrote, "There comes a critical moment when everything is reversed, after which the point becomes to understand more and more that there is something which cannot be understood." This is perhaps the best way of describing what happened to Thomas as he said Mass: he arrived at the critical moment of reversal. Having pursued knowledge all his life, he relaxed, let go, and surrendered to what one medieval mystic called "the cloud of unknowing."

Just as a fish will never know what an umbrella is for, or an elephant will never understand why anyone would want to take up knitting, there are a great many questions that can't be answered from a human frame of reference. When we are banging our heads against one of those questions, the answer we receive from the Source of all is simply, "Behold!" Behold the vastness, the strangeness, and the breathtaking diversity of the created world.

Chapter 6

DYING ISN'T BAD

What is life?
It is the flash of a firefly in the night.
It is the breath of a buffalo in the wintertime.
It is the little shadow which runs across
The grass and loses itself in the sunset.

—CROWFOOT, BLACKFOOT WARRIOR AND ORATOR

Impermanence makes every moment very precious.

—DEEPAK CHOPRA

No heaven will not ever heaven be
Unless my cats are there to welcome me.

—MARK TWAIN

The Dalai Lama was once asked whether he feared his own death. His first response was "No." Then he smiled, shrugged, and said, "I might feel a little bit scared when the moment actually comes." Animals feel the same way. When faced with an immediate threat, they are scared and they do everything in their power to survive, resisting the threat or fleeing from it. But in the absence of an immediate threat they don't worry about death. The *idea* of death doesn't bother them. They pursue survival because they love life, not because they fear dying.

Humans have a hard time with the idea of death. We know that our own death is inevitable, yet we can't predict when it will come. This combination of inevitability and unpredictability is difficult for us to handle. It strikes us as wrong, even as somehow unnatural. When an unexpected death is reported in the press, it is almost always described as "tragic"—the implication being that it could have been and ought to have been prevented. That God not only permits these "tragedies" to occur, but has created a world in which they are inevitable, is the basis of our mistrust in the whole setup. Death is like a goblin lurking in the shadows, waiting to pounce when we least expect it. The only way to escape our dread of it seems to be to turn on all the lights and try not to glance into that shadowy corner.

To humans, every sign of aging is another step in the direction of death, and many of us stubbornly dig in our heels like toddlers resisting bedtime. Do not get me wrong; I am all for looking good—when I think I look good, I actually feel good, but this is not the issue here. We admire those who resist most successfully—through plastic surgery, hormone replacement, cosmetics, diet, exercise, and the like—saying that they look great. It is especially reassuring when celebrities we remember from our youth look pretty much the same as they did thirty years ago, for the aging of our idols is an uncomfortable reminder that we, too, are aging. Of those who actually look their age, we are likely to say, "They've let themselves go." To let go in the face of mortality is exactly what we believe we are not supposed to do.

From the standpoint of nature, a person who is sixty is not supposed to be as strong or as quick as a teenager; a person who is ninety is not supposed to be "as sharp as a tack"; a mother of five is not supposed to look as if she's never given birth. Animals are not mixed up about this. They look and act their ages, and do so without apology. The aging process makes dying easier for them, and would make dying easier for us too, if we didn't resist it so hard. That's probably *why* we resist it. We don't *want* to make dying any easier.

Carl Jung once observed, "The process of death is the one event of life that is the most heavily pregnant with spiritual potential. Death is psychologically as important as birth. Shrinking away from it is something unhealthy and abnormal which robs the second half of life of its purpose." You can "rage, rage against the dying of the light" when you're young, but if you're still doing so during the second half of life, you are missing the spiritual boat. All of the great spiritual teachers are in accord with Jung on this point. They tell us that to live well, we must live in perpetual awareness and acceptance of our mortality, that unless we acknowledge the impermanence of our lives and the transience of most of our preoccupations, we will not be able to judge what is truly important and what is unimportant.

When we hear this advice, it sounds indisputably true. But what are we actually meant to do with it? Many people interpret it to mean that they must make every moment count, that if they let a year go by without ticking off another item on their "bucket list" they are failing to "live life to the fullest." Time's a-wasting. The awareness of mortality lends a rather manic quality to their lives, a sense of working against a deadline.

As animals know better than we, to truly enjoy life is to live as if you had all the time in the world. There is always time to loll around in the sun, lazily observing the striving of bees. What's the rush? It would appear from their profligate indifference to time that the imminence of death is the very last thing on animals' minds. From their perspective, what is "truly important" is to play when you feel like playing and nap when you feel like napping.

A friend of a friend of mine recently learned that he had a cancerous tumor on his kidney. He was terrified not only of the prospect of dying but of devoting what little time he might have left to going through an arduous, debilitating, and financially ruinous course of treatment. As his wife was driving him to his first consultation with the oncologist, they became mired in heavy downtown traffic. Mike hated being stuck in traffic and in normal circumstances would struggle against it by shifting restlessly from lane to lane, trying to position his car in whichever lane was moving marginally faster than the others. Knowing this, his wife asked him which lane he wanted her to get in. Mike replied, "Who cares? I have spent far too much of my life worrying about traffic. I see now that it isn't important at all."

When they finally reached the doctor's office, the news they received was very good. Though the tumor was indeed cancer, it was a type of cancer that has a very high cure rate. Surgery alone would eradicate it, and insurance would cover the cost. Mike wouldn't have to go through chemo or radiation, and after a week or two of surgical recovery would be good as new.

On the way home, the couple once again had to make their way through downtown congestion. Irritably, Mike began to pester his wife with instructions on how to weave through it. "Traffic has started to bother me again," he admitted. To forget what was truly important, now that his dying had been postponed, came as a great relief. We humans might grudgingly make friends with death once it has put a foot over our threshold, but let's face it—we'd much rather give death the bum's rush.

THE CIRCLE OF LIFE AND ITS DISCONTENTS

On the first day of Lent, Roman Catholics line up to get their foreheads smudged with ashes, as the priest intones, "Dust you are and to dust you will return." Scientifically speaking, it would be more accurate for him to say, "To dust you are constantly returning." Much of what you discard when you empty your vacuum cleaner was once part of your own body: hairs that have fallen from your head, and the skins cells that are one of the primary components of house dust. You probably don't miss them, just as you don't miss the thousands of cells that have died off since you woke up this morning.

Think of where you were on this date seven years ago. The body you had on that day has long since perished, for over a period of seven years, give or take, every cell in the human body dies and is replaced by a new one of the same type. If it weren't for this constant dying, you would look terrible. You would find it impossible to recover from even the most minor illness or injury. The death of the worn-out or damaged parts of you enables newborn cells to make a fresh start. It is no exaggeration to say that if you weren't constantly dying, you would only have a few weeks left to live.

A garden in which no living thing is ever put to death will, in very short order, become one in which nothing but the fiercest weeds will thrive. Some plants need to be pruned or thinned out and others need to be sacrificed altogether for the benefit of the whole. Otherwise none of the plants will receive as much moisture and sunlight as they need to flourish. The decaying of that which has died enriches the soil for the living. Without decay, the land would become a desert. In this sense, a better name for Death Valley would be Deathless Valley. Not much can live there because not much dies there.

Death is how life takes turns with itself. Every living thing is nourished by the death of other living things. The debt one plant or animal owes to the dying of others cannot be paid back directly. Instead, they pay it forward. Each gives its life in turn to nourish something else. The mosquito that has feasted on your blood offers its body to the robin. The robin's song is how the mosquito thanks you. Any living thing that dies to nourish another experiences, at the moment of death, a joyous release of pent-up gratitude. The giving of its life is a celebration of that life, and of all the other lives that have made it possible.

There is more to taking turns than eating or being eaten. Living things must die to make room for other living things. The cells of your body die so that fresh ones can take their place. The death of old trees makes space in the forest canopy for up-and-coming saplings. The periodic thinning-out of any one species is essential to the health of an ecosystem, for when one species begins to succeed to an extent that threatens another, imbalance ripples through the entire system, to the detriment even of the species that appears to be dominating. For an elk in a national park that has become overrun by elk, the quality of life is not good.

One spring day, shortly after buying a new house, I was strolling around the property, taking inventory of what already grew there and making plans for the garden. When I came to a large pine tree, I was startled to hear him speaking to me. This had never occurred with such a startling jolt before. Maybe "speaking" isn't quite the right word, for when trees communicate it is my gut chakra that receives the message, and this one felt almost like a punch. The intentions of this magnificent tree came across to me loud and clear. "Get these things away from me!" the pine tree commanded. He was referring to a tangle of overgrown shrubs situated near his base. The shrubs were vying with the tree's roots and stunting his growth. The situation wasn't optimum for the shrubs, either. In being crowded together and obliged to compete, none of the plants could reach their full potential. The pine wanted all these shrubs removed. His tone was so imperative that I complied immediately, disregarding any possibility I was crazy. Since he was a talking pine, one might have expected a "thank you," but he didn't offer one—at least not at that time. Intent on a will to thrive, no further attention was given me once he had gotten what was needed. By the time the tree was moved to speak again, many years later, I had almost forgotten our earlier exchange.

My beloved Wimsey was about to die and wanted to enjoy the outdoors one last time. He was too weak to go out by himself, so I cradled him in my arms as I walked slowly around the garden he loved to gaze upon while basking in the sunlight from my living-room window. I realized that the next time I carried him outdoors, it would probably be to bury him. In the back of my mind lingered the question of what I would do with his remains after his passing, a concept I had yet to accept; it was just too painful. My life without Wimsey, my constant partner for eighteen years, was still impossible to imagine even knowing his death was imminent. He was my dearest friend in the world, and I was devastated to be losing him. The pine tree chose that moment to make himself heard again. He said, "There is a place here. When it is time, I will take him. You can put him under me."

Trees have long memories. Though he expressed no gratitude at the time, this one had never forgotten the shrub sacrifice that enabled him to flourish. When the moment came that he could give something back, he offered to share the very thing that he had once insisted on having all to himself. I will never know what intuition, what telepathy was involved in the tree understanding my emotional pain, but I believe love, the energetic force that runs the universe, was the conduit to this blessing. In the years of scientific research done by Rupert Sheldrake on ESP, a high number of cases in his database involve telepathy that occurred in response to other's needs.

At this point, you are probably expecting me to ask you to join in a rousing chorus of "The Circle of Life." I'm not going to do that, because I know full well that what I have been saying doesn't make the prospect of your own death any more attractive. It might even be making matters worse. Insofar as it is eaten by anything, your body will be devoured by bugs and worms and bacteria, a prospect that is creepy to think about and strikes us humans as a humiliating plummet from our privileged place at the top of the food chain. Even reminding you that those humble organisms will make their way back up the chain, your remains thus nourishing all manner of beautiful and noble things, probably doesn't help much.

The very circularity of the "circle of life" is part of what bothers people about it. A more honest theme song for humans would be "Is That All There Is?" We can't help but feel that life is meant to *get somewhere*. The very cycle that makes animals feel that their lives are important and meaningful makes humans feel pretty much the opposite. We don't want to think of our human remains as beneficial to other living things, because we don't want to think of ourselves as decaying organisms, period. Nor can we take comfort from the knowledge that our eventual absence from the planet will benefit those still living on it. We would much prefer to think that we are indispensable and irreplaceable.

The central importance of death in nature is what makes us, at some level, hostile to nature. How can we love that which, to all appearances, is literally out to kill us? In a way, you could say that those who want to cut down the rain forest, live in glass towers, and pave over every last inch of the planet are acting in self-defense. Human assaults on the biological are our way of insisting that there is more to us than biology. If we can't achieve immortality, there is at least some perverse satisfaction in erecting garbage heaps that won't biodegrade for the foreseeable millennia.

LIFE AFTER LIFE

The last time I saw my father was in August of 2010. It was the day I was to drive my son to Connecticut, to begin his first year of college. We dropped by my dad's house for a quick visit before setting off. With a twinkle in his eye, Dad handed him a crisp one hundred dollar bill and said, "I am so proud of you; go have some fun on me." We hugged and said goodbye. As we walked out the door, I glanced back, noticing a tear welling up in Dad's eye and a dull ache in my heart. "See you in a week." I said. Though ninety-three, he was in very good health, and I had no inkling that his death was coming any time soon, much less in the next few days. Our parting was affectionate but casual, as occurs between people who see each other frequently, and expect to meet again soon. My son and I were two days into our road trip when I got the news. The suddenness of it devastated me. There was so much more I would have said to him had I known that our offhand goodbye was to be the *final* goodbye. This sense of something left unfinished intensified my grief, for it seemed to me irreparable. What had been left unsaid would be *forever* left unsaid.

When I expressed this to a minister who was trying to comfort me, she told me I was mistaken. She described how, after the death of her mother, she had seen a rainbow that she knew beyond any doubt to have been a personal greeting from her mom, who had always loved rainbows. She said that people who have died have the ability to send such signs to their loved ones, and that I should be on the alert for a sign from my father.

The whole thing sounded a bit woo-woo to me. Maybe you find it funny that someone who quotes talking pine trees would accuse anyone else of being woo-woo, but I am, after all, trained in science and the skepticism that goes with it. The notion that someone who has died could influence a natural phenomenon such as a rainbow struck me as outlandish, however much I might wish that it were possible. The skeptic in me came out in full force. I was terrified that hoping for such a thing would just set me up for disappointment. So I shrugged it off, saying, "Anyway, if Dad sent a sign, it would have to be a blue jay, so just don't think about it." And I didn't.

During one of my daily backyard explorations the summer I was eleven, I had stumbled upon a fallen nest. Nearby were five baby blue jays, still baldish and helpless-looking. I knew their parents personally, for blue-jay couples tend to nest in the same area for several years running, and I had come to recognize this pair. At first the parents shrieked and attempted to dive-bomb me in defense their young. But when I persisted in my effort to rescue the babies, they gradually realized that my intentions were friendly and hovered around solicitously, letting me know that they were grateful.

When my father came home that evening, I showed him the temporary nursery I'd created out of a cardboard box and asked for his help. Some parents might try to protect a child from heartbreak by pointing out the unlikelihood of the birds' survival, but my father shared my enthusiasm for the mission, and seemed confident of my ability to pull it off. He found me an eyedropper so that I could feed the little ones the baby formula I'd improvised: mashed up bugs and worms diluted with tap water. It worked. When the fledglings grew big and strong enough to leave the cardboard nursery and rejoin the outdoor "club," I was thrilled. I had long felt that the animals were taking care of me, and now I was discovering that I could take care of them in return. My innocent astonishment at my ability to help creatures in nature was obvious to Dad, and also infectious—he encouraged me every step of the way. My father's delight in this achievement made me feel truly recognized by him. It is my happiest childhood memory.

"It would have to be a blue jay," I said to the minister. The unlikely unfolding of such a sign from my father just made me feel sadder.

After the funeral, I went to Scotland to visit my daughter, who was studying at the University of St Andrews. On October 10, I returned to my home, where a box that had belonged to my father awaited me. It was the last of his personal effects to sort through. He'd kept the box next to his bed, and I'd never known what it contained. Inside I found an assortment of personal memorabilia: photos, newspaper clippings, letters, and such. The following day, I carried this treasure into my conservatory to study the various items more carefully, sitting on the pine bench next to the window. I sat reading by the early autumn sunshine that poured in through the window. I was especially touched to find a bundle of love letters my parents had exchanged when my dad was in the army, during World War II. I spent several hours on that bench, reading through what I was certain Dad considered his great treasures. I was completely engrossed in the story of my parents' early years together. Among the photos, yellowed newspaper clippings, and letters was a note from my mother written on their first wedding anniversary. I noticed it was dated October 11. Startled, I looked up, realizing "Wow, that is today; it is October 11." Taking in the coincidence, I looked toward the window and at that moment, I saw a blue jay perched on the shrub just outside. He was no more than ten inches from the glass, and he was staring at me intently, first with one eye and then with the other. He remained there for several more minutes, never taking his eyes off me, as if wanting to make good and sure that I recognized him.

Was it the ache of regret still lingering inside me for not being present when my dad passed on that precipitated this divine choreography? I will never know. It was beyond anything I would have dared to wish for. One thing is certain: I got the message loud and clear. Thanks, Dad.

In the film *The Sixth Sense,* a little boy who is able to communicate with ghosts confides, "They don't know that they are dead." This reflects a frequent experience of people who have lost a loved one: they will have a recurring dream in which the loved one insists that he or she is not really dead. Though such dreams are very common, they tend to be dismissed by those who have them as mere wish fulfillment. Since the dream is telling them what they most want to hear, they assume it can't be true.

I believe that the dead "don't know that they are dead" because, from their perspective, they *aren't* dead. They are still conscious, still feel pretty much like their old selves, and still care very much about the living. That they are being mourned unnecessarily—or at least to an extent that strikes them as disproportionate—is frustrating to them. When some of them engage in haunting behavior—making things go bump in the night—it is as if they are saying, "What do I have to do to convince you that I'm not dead?"

It's not that they haven't really died. We have, after all, witnessed their burial or cremation. It's just that death isn't quite the big deal we imagine it to be from this side. The body, which is absolutely essential on Earth, is, on their side, of negligible importance. Indeed, they often disclose to the living experiences that we would have thought to be body-dependent, such as an interest in food, or a desire to embrace someone they love.

In my intuitive contacts with animals, I find it often difficult to tell the difference between those who are currently incarnate and those who have died, because the latter continue to manifest the qualities that were once expressed by their animal bodies. Cheetahs are still fast, and tortoises are still slow. Ostriches still feel like they have wings and still can't fly with them. These qualities are a divine idea that, for a time, shapes the physical, yet doesn't depend on the physical. When the body dies, the idea persists, living on just as happily in the divine idea that creates the Earth.

Animals, too, send signs to the living. The night Wimsey died, I suddenly felt an overwhelming desire to listen to music and randomly chose a CD already in the queue. The first to play was Kenny Loggins' "Cody's Song," a hauntingly beautiful tribute to unconditional love. Instantly Wimsey's overwhelming loving presence enveloped me, directing the words of the song straight into my heart, and offering a promise that he would continue to live in the music of my heart. I clearly understood his message coming through the song to dry my eyes, try to smile, and remember that whenever I need him all I have to do is go into the quiet, listen inside, and he will always be there for me. And Wimsey has kept that promise.

I once attended a lecture by the psychic Patricia Mischell. I had arrived late, so I was sitting in the back row of the packed auditorium when Patricia began to contact whatever spirits happened to be in the room. "I seem to be picking up a cat," she said, with surprise. "This is unusual in a gathering—picking up an animal so clearly." As she spoke she moved down the aisle, trying to identify where the cat was coming from—by then I knew what was happening, and she eventually stopped about ten feet from where I sat. "His name is Whi—Whippy?"

"Wimsey," I corrected. Wimsey went on to say hello and to talk a little about our relationship. He then asked Patricia to tell me that my daughter was going to study abroad when she got older. I was not sure at the time why Wimsey thought that it was important to mention her education, but it turned out to be true. Remembering he left this world on her birthday, it began to make sense later on.

People brought up in shamanistic cultures don't doubt the dreams or other signs that they are sent by those who have died. To them it seems that their ancestors are still very much present and can be called upon for help and advice. That is why people in these cultures are able to find comfort and meaning in the circle of life. They can see that dying doesn't mean total annihilation; it just means taking turns.

Animals perceive the world the same way. They are able to sense the presence of the departed. I was going to say that animals conclude from this that their own deaths won't be so bad, but that's not quite right. Animals don't ask the question in the first place, because the answer is, to them, so obvious. What puzzles them is why the same thing isn't obvious to us, why we are so perverse as to doubt the reassurances that the departed keep sending us.

Like humans, I believe departed animals are able to remember what the moment of dying is like. It is my understanding that prey animals do feel scared while they are being pursued by a predator. The fear comes from resistance, and resistance is necessary: otherwise all living creatures would go belly-up at the first sign of danger and not do what they need to do to survive. But for animals, it is not a spiritual fear—not a fear of total annihilation—so once they realize that survival will not be possible, they give up struggling. Prey animals are assisted in this by their predators, who act swiftly and decisively to make the outcome clear, and relatively painless. At this point, we might wonder if they experience what psychics say humans experience as they leave the body behind. Do they step out of their body when a predator swiftly strikes, like we step out of our clothes when getting ready for bed?

We are fascinated by what humans report when brought back to life after they have been pronounced clinically dead. Many describe hovering over the scene, watching with detachment as doctors frantically try to revive them. They report being indifferent to the outcome, or even rather hoping that the doctors will fail, because what happens when they separate from the body feels so wonderful.

A common thread in the thousands of such accounts that have been recorded is a warm and embracing reception by beings on the other side. Sometimes these beings are loved ones who have died earlier;

sometimes they are religious figures such as angels, or Buddha or Christ; sometimes it's a combination of the two. But no matter who is on the reception committee, they convey a feeling of unconditional love, acceptance, and reassurance. Even people whose religions have taught them to expect judgment when they die don't encounter it. No matter what a life has been like, the beings on the other side seem to regard it as an unqualified success. The only bad news they ever convey is the message that the person who has just died needs to go back to the body, that her life isn't finished yet. People who have returned from such sojourns usually say that they have done so reluctantly at first, and that once they get used to being incarnate again, their lives are forever changed for the better. They not only lose their fear of death, but regard it as something to look forward to, a big treat awaiting them after they finish up whatever they've returned to do. A remarkable book, titled *Proof of Heaven: A Neurosurgeon's Journey into the Afterlife*, written by Eben Alexander, MD, a highly trained academic neurosurgeon associated with Harvard Medical School, is a must-read for anyone interested in human near-death accounts.

What we humans find unacceptable about death when we consider it in the abstract *shouldn't* be accepted because it isn't true. Dying doesn't put an end to consciousness; just ask Eben Alexander. It doesn't stop you from being you. The Source of all continues to love you into existence. It's just a different kind of existence. Except for the glimpses of it that people have when they flatline, and the sketchy reports we get from departed people and animals, we don't know much about it. But from what these reports tell us, we have every good reason to believe that we will like what happens to us when we die.

PRACTICE DYING

Animals don't know exactly what will happen when they die any more than we do. In the absence of specific knowledge, they simply trust. They trust death the way they trust life: as participation in the Source. What will happen when they die must be okay because what is happening *now* is okay.

Nothing in animal consciousness corresponds to the distinction humans make between mortal and eternal. They experience the eternal *in* the mortal. Death is an expression of life, and life is an expression of the Source. The Source is within them and all around them. It is what they are made of and what everything else is made of. The thought that it could ever end, or that their connection to it could ever be severed, is nonsensical to them. They wouldn't know how to picture that if they tried.

We humans can only picture it by looking at ourselves from the outside, as we are so inclined to do. If you look at yourself from the outside, you can be certain that what you are seeing is not going to last. It is *already* not lasting. The more you try to stand outside yourself and see yourself as an object, the more you are likely to dread death. The imperishable part of you can only be experienced when you are on the inside looking out.

If you'd like a taste of what animal consciousness is like, here's a simple exercise you can try. Close your eyes for a moment and bring your awareness inside. Experience the rhythm of your breathing and whatever other bodily sensations are happening at the moment. Then open your eyes. Look out at the world. Simply let your eyes absorb whatever is front of them. Experience that first flash of attention—the pure attention that occurs before you go on to name what you perceive or to form various thoughts about it.

Attention is not the eyes that are perceiving, nor is it even the brain that is receiving the impressions from your eyes. It is that which notices what the eyes and the brain are doing. That attention is *you*. It has no content of its own, yet it is as unique as a fingerprint. It is the part of you that is imperishable. Dying won't stop it, even for a second. Dying will simply be the thing that it is noticing.

Saint Francis of Assisi concluded his famous Prayer for Peace with the line, "It is in dying that we are born to eternal life." The conventional interpretation of that line is that dying is how we get to heaven, that eternal life begins *after* death. Yet in his equally famous poem, "The Canticle of the Sun," Francis includes "Sister Death" among the life forces that he hails as his brothers and sisters: the sun, the moon and the stars, earth, air, fire, and water. He praises Sister Death as someone he already knows intimately. He loves Sister Death because she has *already* put him in touch with eternal life: what the animals (and I) call the "Source." St. Francis wasn't worried about his death because he was on friendly terms with the dying that was already happening.

The fear of death is essentially a fear of losing control, and we meet Sister Death in anything and everything that we would like to control but can't. She makes her presence felt in the losses, failures, disappointments, and hassles of our daily lives. She is there when you lose a favorite piece of jewelry, there when your TV suddenly stops working, there when your barbecue gets rained out, there when you realize that the ten pounds you worked so hard to lose have come back. Your response to these minor setbacks is a snapshot of where you currently stand with her. How do you feel when things like that happen? What do you conclude? Do you blame yourself? Blame others? Redouble your efforts to prevent such a thing from ever happening again? Chances are you respond to the prospect of physical death with the same cluster of feelings, conclusions, and strategies.

As Francis taught, you can make friends with Sister Death by befriending the little deaths that occur from day to day. Each one is a reminder that what you think you have attained doesn't last, that even when you get what you want, you can't hold on to it forever. You can come to regard that reminder as helpful, for when you surrender gracefully to it, it brings you back to your connection with Source. Whatever you lose carries you home to that which you cannot lose.

St. Francis took this a step further: he gave up control on purpose. He cultivated his trust in Source by making no effort whatsoever to manage his life. You don't need to go to the extremes Francis went to with this. Source is so eager to connect with you that it will come flooding joyously into your awareness if you give it the slightest opening.

For starters, try picking something you find to be a minor but frequent source of stress. The stress comes from your effort to remain in control. See if you can give up that effort on purpose. Decide that you are not going to rush during rush hour, or not going to get upset that your kid's room is a mess, or not going to check the market reports every day to see how your investments are performing. Or think of something you do frequently out of a sense of obligation, and consider not doing it. Do you really need to reach for your phone each and every time it rings? Does your kitchen really need to be so immaculate that open heart surgery could be performed on the counters? Will anyone really care if your shoes don't match your outfit? If you have been believing that one of these minor obligations is essential, remind yourself that there isn't an animal in the world who would agree. There isn't an animal in the world who could begin to comprehend what all your fuss is about. Let the animals teach you how to become as blissfully oblivious to these concerns as they are.

When you have succeeded in letting go of a trivial preoccupation or two, your awareness will begin to expand into the deeper sources of stress in your life, the bigger uncontrollable things that you have been at pains to control. For me, one of those big uncontrollable things was what other people think of me. When I was called a "vegetarian veterinarian" I died a little inside. I realized how helpless I was to make other people take me seriously, and I minded. I minded very much. Yet the realization that there was really and truly nothing I could do about it was hugely liberating. Animals couldn't care less what anyone thinks of them. In letting go of my own obsession with how I appeared, I came much closer to the happiness they feel. I died a little on purpose, and in dying discovered how St. Francis could think of death as his beloved sister.

SADNESS IS PART OF THE HAPPINESS

I hope I haven't been giving you the impression that you're not supposed to feel sad about death. I was very sad when my father died, and very sad when Wimsey had to go. My life's work has been to prolong the lives of animals and I feel awful on the many occasions when I am unable to do so.

Dying isn't so bad for those who die, but it can be a real bear for those who survive them. Animals feel this too. Most mourn their dead, and a few take it even harder than we do. The famously long memory of elephants makes their grief when they lose a loved one very deep and very long. Like people, many animals regard other individual animals as irreplaceable. They may be inconsolable when they lose a mate, one of their young, or a close friend.

Animals may become inconsolable at the loss of their beloved human companions, as was the case of Greyfriars Bobby, a Skye terrier, who lived with his owner in Edinburgh, Scotland. Bobby's owner died in 1858, was then buried in Greyfriars churchyard, and for fourteen years, Bobby lay on the grave of his master, refusing to leave. The people of the town took pity on him and provided food every day. Today there is a monument to the loyal Bobby at the corner of Edinburgh's Candlemaker Row.

There is a beautiful story about the poet Rumi and animal devotion. In his last years, Rumi was a companion to a favorite female cat who adored him and whom he adored. She was on the bed when Rumi was dying, and at the moment of his leaving his body she gave a great howl, jumped off the bed, ran and hid herself, and starved herself to death. When Rumi was lowered into his magnificent grave, his cat, by order of his daughter, was placed on his heart because as she said, "my father was a friend of all creation."

For humans, the loss of an animal companion can be especially hard. The love we feel for them is at once very physical, and very tightly woven into the fabric of our daily lives. When animals are gone, we miss their body warmth, their smell, the feel of their coat, the sensation of their rough tongue or cold nose or silky ears, the sound of the joyful noises they make unto the Lord. We also miss the routines we share, the morning walk, the jubilant greeting when we come home, and the lap-sitting after dinner that bring a familiar and comforting rhythm to our days. We even miss the hassles: the flea treatments, the picking up of poop, the need to hurry home when our animal has been left alone all day or to find a caretaker when we are going out of town. These inconvenient responsibilities endow our lives with a sense of meaning and importance that we might not notice until gone.

Grieving the loss of a loved one—whether human or animal—is not only permissible, it is essential. When we mourn the loss of physical existence we are paying tribute to the beauty and meaning that is to be found in the physical, the miracle of bodily life on Earth. The fact that we are eternal spiritual beings doesn't detract from the importance of our temporary physical existence. On the contrary, it makes that existence all the more precious and remarkable.

The more we love someone, the more specific he or she becomes to us. At first we may be drawn to a particular breed of dog and admire the individual dog we have adopted for the qualities he has in common with that breed. As we come to know him better, we begin to perceive qualities that distinguish him from his breed. In a pack of beagles we would have no trouble at all picking out *our* beagle. The more we love, the more we come to see the beloved as unique, and the more unique, the more irreplaceable. Our recognition of uniqueness is part of what *creates* the uniqueness. A person or an animal is a center of consciousness that only comes to know itself in being known by another. In a sense, we love individuality into being—and never more so than when we mourn its death. The grief we feel when a fellow creature dies is the love that creates the world.

Humans have rituals to honor the individuality of departed humans and console their survivors. The lack of these rituals is part of what makes the death of animals so hard for people who love them. Often the only ceremony is the signing of papers authorizing the vet to put an animal to sleep—in itself a devastating thing to have to do.

Preparing to honor a companion animal whose death is imminent is as important as planning the funeral of a human. Think in advance about what you will want to have in the way of mementos. Take photos or videos of your beloved animal companion, maybe even have him portrait painted. In a journal record your favorite memories of your friend, or fill a keepsake box with objects that remind you of him—a collar and tags, a favorite toy, the pillow you once scolded him for chewing. Many vets offer soft disks of clay that can be used to take an impression of your animal's paw, then hardened in the oven. You might also want to create a memorial: a tree or shrub or statue in your garden or a little shrine within your house. You could make a charitable donation in your animal's name, just as you would in a departed human's.

When you are missing your animal, writing her a letter or a poem can be very consoling, and may help you to open communication across death's threshold.

It is important to be present when a companion animal is being put to sleep. To be held and stroked and spoken to softly as they leave this world is as comforting to an animal as it is to a person. Dealing with distraught humans can complicate what is already an upsetting procedure; however, veterinarians and their assistants are experts at helping people through the process. Do not feel ashamed to express your grief to these professionals—they understand and will guide you through. Sometimes a human companion decides that being present for the euthanasia of his or her animal companion is just too much to bear. In some clinics, volunteers take the place of humans who are too distressed to comfort their own animals. If you are for any reason unable to be present for your animal's death, being present for one who is a stranger to you may help you with your grief, and will most certainly help both that animal and his or her human friend. Being present when your animal companion leaves this life is extremely important. It may be difficult, but I promise, you will be glad you offered this gift of support and love.

FIRST THINGS LAST

When I outlined this book, the chapter on death seemed like the logical place for it to end. Yet it could also have been the beginning. Death is as much an overture as it is a conclusion to the other themes the animals wanted me to write about. It is in facing death that we realize how much we don't know and how little we really need to know it. It is in overcoming our fear of death that we discover that we are already living in Paradise. It is in coming to love death as a sister that we begin to know how much we are loved in return.

Rumi wrote:

All day I think about it, then at night I say it.
Where did I come from,
And what am I supposed to be doing?

I have no idea.
My soul is from elsewhere, I'm sure of that,
And I intend to end up there.

When I die, I intend to end up at Rainbow Bend. I won't need to notify the post office of a change of address, for it's where I'm already living.

PART III

The Connection of All Creatures

Chapter 7

How to Connect Telepathically with Animals
A Practical Guide

When we love and spend a lot of time with any being—whether an animal or another person—we usually have a pretty good idea of what that person is feeling, and why. I do not believe that people who call themselves "animal communicators" are significantly more gifted in this regard than regular people. I personally do not like the term *animal communicator*, because it infers that someone who is labeled "animal communicator" has a special talent or gift that you do not have. We all come into this world wired to connect with all life.

When I need to know what's going on with an animal who seems troubled, I first rely on my veterinary training, what the animal's human guardian reports, and what my physical senses tell me, as well as my "sixth sense" that all living beings are born with. An intuitive exchange with an animal starts like any other—with physical cues—body language and gestures. From there we reach out from the silent language of our hearts; love creates alignment with human and nonhuman beings. All life responds to offerings of respect, gentleness, admiration, and reverence. To do psychic or telepathic readings of individual animals is not my intention here and is something I've never seen as necessary or desirable. It is not what I will be teaching you to do in this chapter.

Whereas a psychic reading is an attempt to discover otherwise undisclosed information about its subject, my intuitive exchanges with animals are exchanges between equals, companions, about matters of mutual spiritual concern. Say, for example, I have an inner encounter with a dog in a rescue shelter. I probably won't find out how the dog came to be a stray or who his previous people were. Instead I may learn the sort of thing a human survivor of a traumatic experience would share during a deep and searching conversation about the meaning of adversity. Or say that I myself am going through a difficult time. The spirit of an animal may come to comfort me and offer me some wisdom. The inner encounters I have with animals—and will be teaching you to have—are exchanges of *meaning*.

I've been able to connect with animals in this way ever since I was a small child. Nobody taught me how, and there was no particular technique to it. I was just doing what came naturally to me, exercising what I believe to be an ability all of us are born with. Because the ability is seldom recognized or affirmed in our society, most children lose touch with it at a very young age, and forget that they ever possessed it. So why didn't that happen to me? As I mentioned earlier in the book, I felt somehow imprinted in my early years by the animals. My experiences with them in nature are deeply embedded in my core. Animals offered me the validation and interpretive help that children more usually receive from human adults. When they noticed I was open to connect with them, they taught me how to connect more. Also mentioned earlier in the book, scientific research shows that emotional need acts like a magnet in the intuitive process. Emotional needs are expressions of the heart.

Even if you can't remember any instances of it in your own child-hood, I encourage you to think of intuitive, telepathic communication with animals as a natural ability that you once had and have temporar-ily misplaced, rather than as a supernatural power that you are trying to acquire. There is nothing supernatural or paranormal about it. An animal communicator does not possess a gift that you lack.

Now that I am trying to help others to reawaken this capacity, I've had to reflect more about how it works. So let me begin with my thoughts about that. It seems to me that the way in to the mind of any other being is through the mind of the Source. We all exist in the one mind of the Source. Everything in the created world carries a spark of the Source, divine consciousness. It is what all creatures have in com-mon. Though I appear drastically different from an elephant in out-ward form, insofar as we are both manifestations of the divine mind, we are made of exactly the same stuff. What makes an elephant alive is the very same thing that makes me alive. So when I want to experi-ence a spiritual connection with an elephant, I start by connecting to the Source within me. It is the voice of the heart that takes over. As I said earlier, love creates alignment with all creation. Once I connect with that, the corresponding part of another being lies open to me. I don't have to go looking for it. I simply *recognize* it, as one recognizes that which is perfectly self-evident. To be truly recognized is what the Source in every living creature most longs for. Every living creature just eats that up. When you are able to recognize the divine nature of other beings, you become transcendentally charming. Many beings are eager to confide in you.

So the first step in learning to connect with the spirits of animals is to connect to the divine within yourself. To do so, you need to quiet the mundane chatter of your mind and bring your attention into the present moment. I'm going to offer you a variety of practices that might help you to achieve that. You might already do some meditation or other practice that reliably gets you to an inwardly quiet and receptive place. If so, feel free to substitute that for my suggestions.

Practice #1: The Wildlife Photographer

Imagine that you are a wildlife photographer in quest of a close-up. You need to be very quiet and still so as not to frighten away the creature you wish to photograph. At the same time, you need to remain alert so that you will be ready to act as soon as that creature comes near. In a quiet place where you will be protected from interruption, settle yourself in a position that feels both relaxed and alert. Imagine that your thoughts are audible. The more long-winded and complicated a thought, the louder it is. If you become totally carried away with your thoughts, you will scare away the animals for sure. At the same time, imagine that when you exhale, you are creating a blanket of silence. Whenever you notice that your thoughts are becoming noisy, bring your attention to your out-breath to cancel the sound of them. The object here is to quiet the mind rather than to empty it entirely. Thoughts will continue to arise, but you can reduce the noise level by letting go of each thought and bringing your attention back to the out-breath.

Variation: Try this practice in an outdoor setting: your backyard, a park, or a nature preserve. See if you can become so inwardly quiet and outwardly still that the creatures around you are undisturbed by your presence and emboldened to come closer to you than they normally would come to a human being.

Practice #2: Bringing Your Attention into the Present

A quality all animals have in common is that their attention is completely focused on whatever they are doing in the present. Animals don't multitask. They don't make plans for the future or dwell on what happened in the past. In order to connect with an animal mind, your mind needs to be focused on the present moment as well. Here are some simple exercises for focusing your attention:

1. Eat a meal the way an animal does, concentrating on the act of eating without doing anything else. Don't read, watch

TV, listen to music, or converse. Experience the meal with all of your senses. Whenever you notice your mind starting to wander, gently bring it back to your food and to the activity of eating.

2. Often when we are driving, we experience the roads as an entirely manmade environment, constructed for our own convenience. But even in big cities, our roads cut through the habitats of other creatures—often to their peril. (Over a million squirrels are killed each year by vehicles.) Try driving as slowly as the law allows, remaining conscious that there are other creatures all around you, whether you are able to see them or not, and that you are passing through their territories. Be alert to the possibility that an animal may suddenly dart across the road, unaware of the potential danger because animals don't interpret the road the way you do. Considering the road from an animal standpoint will make you a safer driver.

3. Animals experience the world directly through their physical senses, and many of them are gifted with senses that are more acute than ours. Choose one of your physical senses and spend five minutes experiencing your environment with that sense alone. For example, if you choose the sense of smell, focus entirely on the odors and scents around you, noticing those that seldom come to your full awareness. Next time you do the exercise, choose a different sense. Try this practice both indoors and outdoors.

4. If you have a dog, go for a walk together, letting the dog set the pace and choose the direction. Focus your attention entirely on whatever interests your dog from moment to moment. Try to keep the leash loose, so that neither you nor your dog experience any tugging or jerking. In order to do this, you will need to fall into a rapport, anticipating each other's movements. Think of the leash as a symbol of your connection with your dog rather than as the physical means of staying connected. This is a terrific way of

learning to concentrate your attention, and of discovering what the world is like from your dog's point of view.

Practice #3: A Day of Silence

Silence is often practiced in the context of a spiritual retreat, but I find the practice even more powerful when it is incorporated into my ordinary life at home. What keeping silent means is to refrain entirely from the use of words—neither speaking, hearing, reading, nor writing them. (By this definition, animals live their whole lives in silence, even though they make sounds.) As you settle into silence, you will probably find that your attention gradually shifts away from verbal thoughts and toward sense impressions, emotions, and mental images. In this way, your consciousness becomes more like that of an animal. This is a wonderful practice to share with an animal companion, if you have one. If you normally use words to communicate with your animal, refrain from doing so on this day.

OPENING THE HEART

Once your mind is quiet and attentive, the next step in connecting to the divine within you is to open your heart. We are most likely to feel that our hearts are open when we feel warm, expansive, and loving. But if you are not already in that place, trying to get there on purpose doesn't always work, and your effort can backfire into a sense of personal inadequacy. So when you work with the heart-opening practices, start from the premise that your heart can do no wrong. Whatever it is feeling—or not feeling—is true, sincere, and of value. Let your heart decide which of the practices it feels like doing at any given moment, and let it decide when to quit. Don't try to force a result, and don't evaluate. Whatever happens (or doesn't happen) is fine.

Practice #4: The Keepsake Box

Picture a beautiful box in which you store mementos of love, compassion, and kindness that you have received over the years. Search your memory for items to place in this box. For example, recall a time when:

- someone made you feel completely understood and accepted
- someone really knocked him- or herself out to help you
- you received a gift that was far more generous than you expected, and exactly what you had been wanting
- you did something hurtful and the other person fully forgave you
- you were feeling worthless and received a sincere and glowing compliment
- you couldn't meet some obligation and another person let you off easy

As each memory comes to mind, picture holding it at heart level and notice what happens. If you feel a stirring of warmth or joy or genuine gratitude, place the memory reverently in your imaginary keepsake box. If you're not feeling it, set that memory aside. (Don't tell yourself that you should be feeling something that you don't truly feel.) Each time you return to this practice, begin by taking out and appreciating the items that you have previously placed in the box. Then add any new mementos that might come to mind.

We are most easily moved to gratitude when we have received a gift or a favor that we have done nothing to earn or deserve. Having awakened gratitude by recalling specific incidents like those listed above, see if you can extend the feeling to the blessings all of us receive every day—blessings that no one has to earn or deserve. We are blessed by the sun and the rain, the moon and the stars, the trees, and the flowers. We are blessed by the firm earth under our feet, the air we breathe, the water we drink and bathe in, and the warmth of our own blood. Even when nothing in your life is going the way you want it to go, you wake up every day to find yourself in this miraculously beautiful and supportive environment, and you get to live in it for free! Bring all of this to mind, and bask in the awareness of your good fortune.

Practice #5: Receiving an Animal's Appreciation

If you have a companion animal, do something that makes that animal demonstrably happy. Get your cat to purr or your dog to jump up and down with joy. Bring the whole of your attention to the gratitude your animal is expressing. Think: "This is the God within me being praised." Learning to fully take in the appreciation your animal bestows is particularly helpful if you're the sort of person who has trouble accepting compliments or thanks that come from other people.

Practice #6: The Noah's Ark of Emotions

Animals have a unique ability to touch the human heart. In fact, sometimes animals move us when nothing else will.

Imagine you have built an ark and need to populate it with all the different ways of feeling moved by an animal. Think of a story, a picture, a film clip, or a memory of an animal that moves you in a particular way: an animal who makes you laugh; one for whom you feel compassion; one who inspires awe and admiration; one who makes you go all mushy with affection. For the purpose of this practice you might want to create a physical collection: a file of pictures, anecdotes, and/or video clips. Return to your ark periodically, either singling out a particular item that evokes an emotion you want to feel at that moment, or just browsing to reexperience the various feelings you've had in the past. This practice can be especially helpful at times when you're caught up in thoughts and out of touch with your heart.

Practice #7: The Heart on a Bad-Hair Day

Mystics and seers who are able to connect with spiritual beings usually advise detaching somewhat from the physical senses and the emotions. Since the spiritual beings don't have bodies and aren't very emotional, putting oneself in a neutral and somewhat disembodied state helps one to establish a rapport with them. Some people find that they can't do this at all, and a great many people find that they are unable to do it at the very times when hearing from them, or perhaps a guide or an angel (or from God), would be most welcome. When we're sick or exhausted or in the grip of some powerful and painful emotion, input from above might really help, yet we feel we are in no fit state to present ourselves at the gates of heaven.

This is what's so great about animals as spiritual helpers. They're incarnate just like us. They know what it's like to feel needy or threatened or sad. When you're having a bad-hair day, spiritually speaking, you don't need to tidy yourself up to connect with an animal. On the contrary, the strong emotion that makes it impossible for you to quiet your mind or fill your heart with love and light can become the very means of connection.

The next time you are in the grip of some strong emotion that makes it impossible for you to do any of the previous exercises, don't fight it. Instead, bring the whole of your attention to what you are feeling. What you want to experience is the texture and sensation of the emotion itself, as opposed to the many thoughts you are probably having about the emotion. You want to experience the emotion through the body more than the head. For example, if you are anxious, your mind is probably full of worries and problem-solving schemes. If you are angry, your mind is probably busy replaying the incident that set you off or engaged in self-righteous diatribes. Instead, you want to focus on what anger or anxiety feels like on a physical level. Notice what part of your body feels it the most, and what the sensation is like. Instead of trying to get rid of that sensation, say "hello" to it and keep it company for a few minutes. Whenever your mind starts to veer off into anxious or angry thoughts, gently bring it back to what is happening in your body.

As you are simply sitting with the difficult feeling, invite an image of an animal to come. This may or may not happen. Don't try to force it. Simply invite it and see what happens. Should an animal image appear, recognize the emotion you are feeling as your connection to it. This animal knows how you feel, and you know how she feels, because all living creatures experience emotion. You are not isolated in your distress. On the contrary: it connects you to something universal. *All* feelings are an expression of our aliveness, and a manifestation of the God within.

WORKING WITH THE IMAGINATION

Most of us are used to thinking that "imaginary" is the opposite of "real." That is, when we imagine things, we are just making them up. In the spiritual life, though, there are some realities that cannot manifest unless we begin by imagining them.

Think of it like throwing a party. You send out invitations, decorate your home, stock up on refreshments, and maybe even hire some entertainers. In doing so, you are creating an artificial situation, for in the absence of such exertions, a party is unlikely to "just happen." Yet once you've done your bit and the party is in full swing, what goes on to happen is natural, spontaneous, and real.

Imagining is one of the best ways of inviting beings to manifest to you on an inner level. It's how you let them know that they are welcome to appear. For example, you might do a guided visualization in which you picture yourself coming upon a wise, old hermit in a forest. To begin with, you are just making this up. In your mind, you design a costume for your hermit and a hut for him to live in, and you think up things for him to say when the two of you first meet. But if you persist in this, you may find that something starts to happen that you yourself do not seem to be inventing. The hermit expresses some idea you've never thought of before, something that comes as total news to you. When that occurs, it may be because an actual spiritual being has come along and taken over the hermit role, donning the costume and making himself at home in the setting you created for him. Instead of inventing the whole story on your own, you and this other being are now collaborating on it. The guided fantasy was like getting ready for a party, and now an actual guest has shown up.

The reason it works this way is that spiritual realities are too abstract and ephemeral to be readily apprehended by incarnate people. Our minds tend to wander away from them and toward something more concrete. When we fantasize or visualize, we are inviting other minds to make themselves known in a form that we can wrap our own minds around. In effect, we are saying to someone invisible, "Put on this costume so that I can see you." We can use imagination in the same way to connect with the spirits of animals who are not physically present—both those who are currently incarnate in some other location, and those who have passed on.

Practice #8: Creating an Imaginary Animal Sanctuary

When I was a little girl, I invented the imaginary place introduced earlier, Rainbow Bend. (The name was inspired by the song "Somewhere Over the Rainbow.") It was (and still is) my own personal sanctuary where, in my imagination, I entertain animals that I knew and liked. It is also where all animals I know who have passed are invited to play and live. I imagined this place so vividly as a child that it has gone on existing all my life, attracting the spirits of actual animals. When I want to get in touch with an animal who is not physically present, Rainbow Bend is where we meet up.

The practice is to dream up your own animal sanctuary. Because it is located outside the physical plane, it doesn't have to follow the physical laws we have on Earth (unless you want it to). You can, if you wish, have parrots and penguins living side by side. Set it up however you like, imagining it vividly and in great detail. Create plants and topography and weather. Build in features that will delight particular animals: a mountain of nuts for the squirrels, a great pile of logs for the beavers, a patch of smelly grass for the dogs to roll around in. Experience this place with all of your physical senses, creating sounds, smells, tastes, and textures, as well as sights.

Keep returning to this setting over multiple meditation sessions until it becomes so familiar that you can evoke it easily whenever you like. Visit it during different seasons and at different times of the day. You can, if you wish, embellish it over time, adding new features. Observe it carefully each time you revisit it in your imagination. Notice whether any of its features have begun to change on their own.

Once you have established your imaginary sanctuary, begin to invite animals to live in it. They can be animals of your personal acquaintance, or strangers, or both. They can be currently living, or deceased, or both. Each time you invite a new animal, picture yourself in the sanctuary, coming out to welcome it. Picture it being greeted by the animals who already live there. On subsequent imaginary visits, make your rounds, greeting each of your guests and catching up on what's new.

If you find that this practice is working well for you, it makes a good starting place for other meditations. Whenever you wish to contact an animal spirit, you can go to your imaginary place and invite the animal to meet you there. You can also use it as the setting for your mind-quieting and heart-opening exercises.

Practice #9: Imagining Yourself as an Animal

Choose a type of animal that attracts you. Imagine that you've woken up one morning to find yourself in that animal's body. The first thing you notice are features of your new body that your human body didn't have. It might be wings, fins, fur, a trunk, or a tail. In your imagination, explore all the possibilities of that body part, trying out the various things you can do with it. For example, spread your wings, fold them, flap them, fly with them, groom them.

Once you've explored the most obvious differences, you begin to become aware of parts your new animal body has in common with the human one, and how the animal version is different: for instance, sharper teeth or stronger legs or eyes set on the sides of the face instead of in the front. Experience those differences and their implications. Notice what you can do now that you couldn't do in a human body, and what your human body could do that your animal body can't, and consider how those changes affect you. How will your life be different if you don't have dexterous hands, or if your nose is only six inches from the ground, or if you can breathe underwater but not on dry land? How do the differences change your perceptions, your emotions, and your values?

After doing this practice several times focusing on animals you especially like, try it with an animal you dislike or find repellant.

SENDING TELEPATHIC MESSAGES TO ANIMALS

By quieting the mind, focusing on the present, and opening the heart, we create the sacred space in which our souls can encounter the souls of animals. This is where you should begin whenever you wish to initiate such an encounter. Spend a few minutes doing one or more of the practices described so far, or any other practice that gives you the same result. I find that meditating daily makes it easier to settle my mind and open my heart at will, without having to make a big production of it. The sacred space I want to be in becomes so familiar that to get there is as easy as slipping into my favorite bathrobe.

Having come this far without much difficulty, a lot of people find they lose confidence when it comes time to initiate an actual spiritual encounter. The anxiety is about not knowing what to expect, or expecting too much. Some of the animal contacts in this book express themselves in complete and coherent sentences, and at some length. You're not getting anything remotely like that from an animal, so you figure you must be doing something wrong.

The animal quotations you find in this book are unusual in my own experience, and seem to have come to me in that form *because* I was writing a book. Both the animals and I were making a special effort to rise to this occasion. When not trying to write a book, most of my inner encounters with animals are wordless.

Animals think in pictures and feelings. When they want to connect with you, the most natural way for them to do it is by sending a mental image, a feeling, or both. The fact that I "heard" the words quoted in this book doesn't mean that the animals were sending words. Rather, the words sprang from my own mind spontaneously when I received a mental image or a feeling. If someone sends you a postcard with a picture of a mountain on it, the word "mountain" is almost certain to flash across your mind. Though you weren't sent the word, it nevertheless arrives with the picture. This is what is happening when people quote words "said" by an animal who doesn't actually know any words.

The best way to learn what animal messages are like is to practice sending such messages yourself before attempting to receive any. The "languages" animals use instead of words are languages that humans know too. We're just not accustomed to relying on them.

Practice #10: Sending a Pictorial Message

You can practice this with your companion animal if you have one. When there is something you would like your animal to do, instead of issuing a verbal command, form a mental picture of the desired action. Picture your cat coming to sit in your lap or your dog fetching a favorite toy, then imagine that you are sending that picture over the "telepathic airwaves." You may be startled to discover that your animal actually responds to your mental request. On the whole, companion animals prefer this mode of communication, just as you probably prefer messages in your native language to messages that have to be painstakingly translated from Swahili.

You can also use mental pictures to send messages that are impossible to convey to an animal in words. For instance, if you are leaving on a trip, trying to verbally reassure your animal that you will return in a week is futile. Instead, during your absence, periodically send an image of yourself coming through the door, joyfully reuniting with your animal, and resuming your familiar routine together.

If you don't have an animal companion, go outdoors, notice what creatures are there, and send them "picture postcards" of the sort of thing that might interest them. Send a bee a picture of a garden with lots of flowers to pollinate, or send a raccoon a picture of a dumpster loaded with discarded human food. For the purpose of this exercise, it doesn't matter whether the animals actually receive these greeting cards (though they very well might). You're just trying to get a feel for what it is like to send them.

Practice #11: Sending a Feeling

As with the previous exercise, practicing this one with a companion animal is ideal. This time your task is to send an emotion. Start with one that is directly related to the animal. For instance, instead of saying

"Good dog!" simply experience the emotion of being pleased. Notice what it feels like in your body. It might help to exaggerate the feeling a bit, really filling yourself up with the sense of being pleased. Then send it.

When you find that your animal seems to be responding to emotional messages that directly concern him or her, you can go on to work with sending other feelings that you might be having. You can let your animal know that you feel sad or worried or excited. None of this is going to come as news to your companion. He or she has been picking up on your moods all along, and probably knows what you are feeling even better than you do yourself. That's not really the point. Your purpose is simply to get used to *deliberately* sending feelings. This will help you to recognize feeling messages from animals when you receive them.

Practice #12: Making a Metaphor

A metaphor is a mental image that symbolically communicates a feeling. For example, we may say that we are "drowning in debt." The mental picture isn't meant to convey literal drowning, but the feeling of being overwhelmed by financial obligations.

When you have a strong feeling, sit with it a moment and see if an image comes to mind—an image that expresses the feeling symbolically. This is pretty likely to happen, but if it doesn't, notice whether some familiar figure of speech comes to mind—an expression like "blow my top" or "bursting with pride." Form a literal mental picture of what that figure of speech is saying.

You don't need to send this image to anyone. The purpose of the exercise is simply to learn to express feelings through symbolic pictures so that you will be able to recognize such a message should you receive one from an animal.

Practice #13: Sending Comfort

Some animal-rescue shelters have websites featuring photos and stories of individual animals who are currently up for adoption. You can, if you like, choose one of these individuals to be the beneficiary of this exercise. Or you can, if you prefer, think of a hypothetical animal in a predicament that stirs your compassion: a farm animal facing slaughter, or a wild animal threatened by poachers or by the shrinking of its habitat. Take a few minutes to focus on the pain this animal must be feeling. Then think about what you could offer in the way of comfort. It could be a mental picture, or a feeling, or both. For instance, you could offer an abandoned animal a feeling of being cherished, or a mental picture of being petted and played with. To an animal who is about to die, you could offer a picture of a happy afterlife in your imaginary animal sanctuary. Prepare your offering in your own mind and heart, then send it telepathically.

Practice #14: Sending a Request for Help

When humans need help, we tend to put our request for it in the form of a problem for which the helper could provide a specific solution. We ask questions like "Should I go through with the surgery my doctor is recommending?" or "How can I find a romantic partner?" Such requests for advice are not very intelligible to animals. What an animal is capable of receiving and responding to is the concern or feeling *behind* the question. In emotional terms, "Should I go through with the surgery?" really means, "I am scared to have the operation and also scared of what might happen if I don't have it." "How can I find a partner?" means "I am feeling lonely."

Think of a current problem or concern for which you would like to receive inner guidance. First phrase this request in the form of a question, as you probably would if asking a fellow human for help. Then sit quietly with yourself, exploring the feelings that motivate the question. Put what you are feeling in the form of a statement instead of a question. Notice whether that feeling evokes any mental pictures or metaphors. Then telepathically send your statement—along with the emotion and any images or metaphors that came up—to anyone whose help and guidance you would like to receive. (It could be God, an angel, an animal, or a fellow human being.) When you request help or guidance by expressing the concern behind your question, you are more likely to receive what you truly need—not just from animals, but from other spiritual beings, and even from living people.

ESTABLISHING CONTACT

The previous set of practices has taught you to send various types of messages to animals in a form that is intelligible to them. At the same time, they have familiarized you with the forms in which animals are most likely to connect with you, so that you will recognize a message when you receive one. Now it's time to practice initiating a two-way exchange.

When we try to telephone a fellow human, we don't always connect, even when we've dialed the right number. The callee might be away from the phone or too busy to answer. The same is true of telepathic communication. Animals are busy living their own lives. They're not just sitting around waiting by the "telepathic phone" hoping to get a call from a human. Sometimes you won't get a response at all, and sometimes the response comes belatedly: hours or days later, you hear from an animal who has only just then picked up its "voicemail." So please don't interpret the lack of an immediate response to mean that your efforts to send messages are failing.

Practice #15: Inviting an Animal to Engage with You

This practice is about making yourself approachable and available to whatever animal might wish to make your acquaintance. Though you might be eager to contact a beloved animal companion who has died, the very intensity of your longing is likely to put you and your animal friend under too much pressure. So don't start there. In the beginning, it's best to keep your invitation low-key and open-ended, without feeling attached to a particular result.

Begin by quieting your mind and putting your heart in a receptive place, using whichever practices work best for you. When you feel inwardly ready, invite an animal to be present. Don't specify what individual animal or type of animal you would like to meet. Rather, send out a feeling of welcome to any animal who wishes to show up. Then simply wait, keeping your mind quiet, attentive, and open.

You may find that you are getting a mental image of a particular animal. Or you might get a picture that is a bit more vague. For instance, you might get an image of a body part—a tail or a wing or a fin—without being able to pinpoint exactly what animal it belongs to. If you are not getting a mental picture, check to see whether you might be getting an impression related to a different sense: a sound or a smell or a sensation in some part of your own body. Or you might feel the presence of a particular mood or emotion.

At this point, it may occur to you to wonder whether this mental picture or sensation is coming from a real animal or is just something your own imagination has conjured up. Don't let this worry you. Remember: using our imaginations is how we invite something to manifest that is not merely imaginary.

Think of what it would be like to meet an animal in the wild. Since most animals are initially shy of us—and we of them—you wouldn't immediately try to touch her or pick her up or talk to her or make any kind of demands on her. You would be quiet and gentle and unobtrusive, letting her get used to your presence and make up her own mind whether she wants to engage further. Inward contact with an animal spirit works the same way. At this point, all you want to do is to sit quietly with whatever is manifesting, getting used to her presence and letting her get used to yours.

If the animal wants to engage further, she will let you know. She may come closer, allowing you to touch her in your imagination, or she may gaze steadily at you, which is your invitation to return the gaze. Allow yourself to be satisfied with whatever is offered, without trying to push for more.

Any sense of failure or disappointment with the results of this practice is a sign that you are expecting too much and concentrating too hard. The whole purpose of the inviting practice is to learn to be present without being pushy. If you can be satisfied with an encounter that is very fleeting and ephemeral, satisfied even with nothing happening at all, you're doing well. Learning not to strive for a result is how you become approachable.

You would probably like me to give you instructions on how to develop your inner encounters with animals, once you have learned to invite and perceive their presence. But what happens from this point onward will be between you and them, and up to you and them. Having worked with the practices already given should equip you very well for whatever happens next.

Because such encounters are, by their very nature, so private and personal, they can't be confirmed by the people around you. For this reason, doubts are likely to arise. You may wonder whether you've truly understood what an animal is trying to send you, or whether what you have intuited is actually true. You may even wonder whether the exchange really happened. The next section will give you some suggestions on how to work with these issues.

DOUBT AND DISCERNMENT

Among animal behaviorists, anthropomorphizing is considered the cardinal sin. To anthropomorphize is to project human psychology onto other creatures, attributing human qualities to them and assuming that their emotions and motivations are the same as yours would be if you were in their place. I agree with this; however, as you have read in this book, I believe that many feelings and qualities are common to all living creatures. Still, if we carelessly assume that other creatures are exactly like us, we will miss out on the differences in their perspectives, and what those differences have to teach us.

A similar issue comes up when we attempt to connect with animals telepathically. Are we truly hearing from them, or merely projecting our own thoughts and feelings on them? When we misunderstand other humans, they can set us straight with words of their own choosing. Animals can't do that—at least, not with words. (If we observe carefully, they will often set us straight with their behavior.) The same difficulty crops up with other spiritual beings. For instance, people tend to project their own moral judgments on what they believe is the Source, assuming that the Source disapproves of whatever they themselves disapprove of. When we do that, we lose touch with the true Source of all. We will likewise lose touch with the true spirits of animals if we project ourselves onto them instead of really listening to them.

The difference between listening and projecting is difficult to discern, and nobody gets it right 100 percent of the time. When we make a mistake, we usually discover it retrospectively. That is, we are unaware of projecting at the time we're doing it, but can look back and realize that we were doing it a year ago. By noticing and admitting past mistakes, we gradually learn to perceive more accurately.

Another way to become alert to errors is to make them on purpose. For example, if you want to correct your golf or tennis swing, you can deliberately do it wrong, exaggerating the error until your body learns what doing it wrong feels like, and how that feeling differs from doing it right. That's what the next two practices are about.

Practice #16: Projecting on Purpose

Imagine that you are making inner contact with whatever type of animal you would like to have as a spiritual guide. Picture yourself in the presence of that animal. Then initiate a conversation by asking the animal about some current concern of yours.

When it's time for the animal to answer, make up what he says. Have him express an idea that sounds wise from your own point of view—something you yourself might say when you are at your best. Have the animal express this very persuasively in human terms, perhaps illustrating what he means with an example, or answering possible objections as if he is trying to win an argument. Notice the sensations you have in your body while you are doing this. You may find that there is a subtle feeling of tension or pushiness somewhere in your body. Or you may find that you aren't aware of any bodily sensation because all of your energy seems to be in your head. Pay particular attention to your throat. When we are talking to ourselves in our heads, we often subvocalize—that is, our throats go through the same motions they would make if we were speaking aloud, only less so. There is a very subtle sense of tension, movement, or pushing at the throat level—a sensation that is absent when we are listening to someone else.

Carefully notice what projecting feels like when you are doing it on purpose. Repeat the exercise periodically until you become so sensitized to the feeling that you begin to notice it spontaneously, at times when you are not doing the exercise.

Practice #17: Neutral Listening

Listen to someone you don't know giving information about which you have no strong feelings, neither agreeing nor disagreeing. You could watch a TV program about cooking or home repair where the host is simply giving instructions. Or you could eavesdrop on a conversation of strangers on a topic you don't care about. Notice what happens—and what *doesn't* happen—in your body. This is what simply listening feels like. Contrast this experience with what you experienced in the previous practice.

Practice #18: Receiving a Mystery

Connections, intuitive information we receive from animals—or from any other kind of spiritual being, for that matter—are sometimes cryptic. We flash on a mental image or "hear" a brief phrase whose meaning is not immediately clear to us. When that happens, it is very tempting to go into intellectual overdrive, attempting to analyze and interpret the message. This is a leading cause of getting things wrong. Our intellects can only tell us what we already know—which is probably *not* what the inner being is trying to convey to us. To learn something new from them, we have to be able to receive a mystery, and allow that mystery to unfold at its own pace. What we don't understand when we first receive it needs time to ferment in our subconscious. Sometimes it becomes clear after we've slept on it for a night or two. Sometimes it only becomes clear after months or years have elapsed. The trick is to just leave it alone in the meantime, trusting that the light will dawn eventually, and will likely dawn sooner if we don't overthink. Here's a practice that should help:

Fantasize another encounter with a spirit guide. For this exercise, it doesn't matter whether the guide is human, animal, or some kind of spirit, like an angel. As in Practice #6, initiate a connection by asking a question or raising some current concern of yours. The catch is that your spirit guide is unable to speak. Instead, he or she responds by placing an object in your hand. Don't spend time deliberating about this. The guide responds immediately. The object you are given is the very first one that comes into your mind. Its relevance to your question or concern is unclear, and you are given no explanation. In your imagination, take the object and place it somewhere in your actual home. Then abruptly end the fantasy without giving the object or its meaning any further thought.

Over the coming days, when you pass the spot where you have placed the imaginary object, allow yourself to fleetingly notice it. Picture it very briefly in your imagination, then forget about it again. At some point, the significance of the object and its connection to your question may suddenly dawn on you. Or not. Consider the exercise a success either way, because its purpose is simply to teach you to receive what you don't immediately understand.

Chapter 8

THE ANIMALS SPEAK
FOR THEMSELVES

Ask the animals and they will teach you, or the birds of the air and they will tell you; or speak to the earth, and it will teach you, or let the fish of the sea inform you. Which of these does not know that the hand of the Lord has done this? In his hand is the life of every creature and the breath of all mankind.

—JOB 12: 7-10

A huge part of my motivation for writing this book was to plead the case for the conservation of endangered animals and their habitats, and to raise awareness of the many animals—wildlife and domestic animals, who suffer from human exploitation, cruelty, and neglect. Particularly heartbreaking is the devastating increase of homelessness in our companion-animal population. The problem with acting on this impulse is that it kept resulting in a harangue. You wouldn't have liked reading it, and the animals themselves don't much care for that manner of speaking. They don't like it when we humans get harsh with one another—not even when the harshness is in their defense.

While trying to think of a better approach, my procedure was to settle down and meditate and send out a general intention of deep love. I found by doing this, messages did in fact come. They came in a gentle, loving, compassionate manner I instantly recognized as directly, purely animal heart and soul. What was most striking to me in the connection that flowed was their concern for *human* suffering. In their view, the harm we do to them is a consequence of human misunderstandings that make our own lives as miserable as we are making theirs. They are especially concerned about human loneliness, which they see as an expression of our disconnection from nature and from the Source. (They point out that what humans call "nature" *is* the Source. In their minds, these are not separate concepts.) They feel great empathy with our loneliness, the more so because we are inflicting it on them as well, as our actions shrink their numbers and their habitats. They want us to help them, but they also want to help us.

Another thing the animals wanted to share with humans was their individual species' purposes on Earth. Their own view of this is sometimes strange from a human standpoint and, in the case of the dog, downright funny. (Dogs think they're here to train us.) They give us a glimpse into animal cultures as the expression of divine ideas.

I have been able to receive intuitive messages from animals ever since I was a child, but until rather recently, these encounters rarely came in words. I would pick up feelings and mental pictures mostly, and occasionally a single word or a short phrase. For that matter, I myself was not much of a talker, and writing didn't come easily to me. It was only out of an urgent need to connect with humans on behalf of animals that I buckled down to the task of expressing myself in coherent paragraphs. Connecting became more complex—not in words, exactly, but in a form that I could readily translate into human prose, even if the syntax was a tad peculiar. The words you will read come from me, but the thoughts behind the words come from the animals. At times I use phrases like "what you humans call;" I am hesitating, struggling a bit to find a common English word like "bullet" because there was some puzzlement or confusion mixed in with the mental picture the animal was sending. I search hardest for the names of things that animals find especially foreign.

In the following pages, I will share with you two messages of wisdom from animal ambassadors that I believe speak for all (one representing domestic animals and one representing wildlife). They say better than I what animals want us to know. The first offering is from our companion and best friend, the dog. The other is from the king of all animals, the magnificent white lions.

Dog

I speak as one you call dog. I am alive in body now, but soon I will be moving to spirit, leaving this body behind. It has provided all that has been needed for me to fulfill the purpose of this life, but soon I must move to passing. I have done this many times before. This will be more difficult for my human companions than for me.

Dogs, all of us, are proud and grateful for the bodies we receive coming in to this life. We notice humans think we are beautiful, but it is confusing to us that sometimes you do not like the bodies you have been given as gift in this life. Why do you not love this gift, as we do? We are always learning from humans as you also learn from us.

We have taken on being your companions not because humans are superior, not as "service" to you, not as your entitlement. We, the animals, have taken this on ourselves as part of our development, for we grow in our own spirits through deep loyalty to humans and companionship with them. Know that in the eternal heart what is good and helps self simultaneously is good and helpful to all.

We dogs have become masters of the eternal heart—but this is eternal process, ongoing, there is always more to learn. Such is the way, for no life form is ever "finished" growing or changing. Helping humans connect to eternal heart also helps us: not duty to human but loyalty to human.

The qualities of the eternal heart we offer as a teaching to humans, our gift to you, is like going on a walk together, noticing all we pass along the way. It is not about where we go but about who we are being as we travel. As companions, neither of us takes the lead at all times. We sometimes allow you to lead (which, out of our fierce loyalty to you we put up with, for there is always something for us to learn), and sometimes in your wisdom, you let us lead making our teaching to you easier on all.

Humans are known by us often to require extensive training (my human word). So many of you are alarmingly deficient in the ways of the heart—trust, connection to eternal, that which is ever present, preventing you from "being" joyous in now. We have much to teach you about this.

You are often distracted. You are busy filling in what, to us, is never empty or missing. We watch as you look in empty places for what is already found in the heart. But, we are patient and learn much in relationship with you. Our highest joy is blending with humans who understand heart connection and exist in deepening understanding of giving and receiving—love and devotion. We are eager to help you understand.

Humans easily notice loyalty in dogs. After we leave this life, in spirit, we are often so connected and loyal to our humans that we choose to reincarnate quickly, come back to same family in body of another animal. This allows us to continue walking with you along the path of life.

If you are not sure of this loyalty, if this is new to you, please sit with a dog who loves you or loves someone in your family. Look into her eyes. Do not look with your eyes, ears, or thoughts. Use the eye of your heart; this is where you will find all that fulfills. Dog will reveal the truth of this. Please do not stuff the head with ideas. Be still and receive through heart what dog offers you. She may even "speak" of other lives. Dog "speaks" messages to humans with eyes, vibration of heart center, energy in and around the physical body, body movements, feelings, and bark tone. But, you must receive through the heart. (Dogs communicate easily and efficiently with nonhumans and nature also through smell, but we know smell is very weak and inefficient in humans.) All of this comes easier with practice and keeping us close by to remind.

If it is possible that you do not have this dog to sit with, please find one of us who has no home (there are multitudes of us). They will teach you (if you choose to learn) as they are the best teachers—their hearts cry out to connect and be companions with you. When offered home and companionship, they are the most kind, most gracious, loyal, and wise among us. They have suffered greatly to achieve this wisdom. They are our master teachers—their love will fill in the places you seek to fill by searching in the empty places. They will bring you much joy, and will even heal your physical body. They will teach you the great tragedy, the greatest tragedy of my kind, which is not to have a human companion. We know you also suffer this tragedy in your own kind.

I "speak" now of my boy, my human companion (who is very fast at running for one with only two legs). It is a great blessing to be in companionship with young humans; they easily understand the voice of the heart. I love this boy with all my heart can hold. We bonded as pups, he a human pup, me canine (definitely a human word) with four legs and at the time, bigger, and of course, faster than he. On his bed at night, your sleep time, it was not always easy for me, even when he was small. I sometimes had to fight for my space. His two legs moved all night, pushing my body as he ran and played in what you call dreams.

During our years together, I watched those legs grow long and strong, taking him away more and more to other places. Side by side, we grew big; we played every day. We learned when it was not wise to sleep in certain places, how to play with toys (not eat them), and if it was safe to run away or not. My boy learned how and when to share his food with me. I learned to escape from inside to visit other dogs without breaking doors, upsetting humans. I taught my boy how to find me when I ran away and forgot my way back home. He learned this lesson very well— better than I learned not to run away. I stayed by his side when he felt alone, afraid, and when he needed the touch of my very soft coat of hair, there I was, and still remain.

Now grown and strong, he is away from our group much of my time. He always returns and shows me the love he holds in his heart for me. It is our special place. My being overflows with joy when my companion comes home. Hearing his voice, hearing his laugh—we are back to the place of no time but now. He understands the voice of the heart; I have taught him well. He has taught me too—as much as I know about the sacred bonds of heart, there is always more to learn. The more I wait in patience for the boy to return, the deeper my loyalty and love for him grow.

I am now old, and my body does not move as fast; I no longer run away. I will remain here as long as my companion still needs me and as long as my body will allow. No matter how we both change, wherever we both go—his heart is never disconnected from mine, nor I from his. My boy and I live in each other's heart. Anytime we want to be together we can just go inside and listen.

THE WHITE LIONS

The white lions of Timbavati, rare to begin with, have been hunted almost to extinction. The recessive gene that produces their striking white coloration was at one time believed to render them incapable of surviving in the wild, and was thought to weaken regular lions who interbred with them. This belief provided the rationale for confining them to "canned hunting" preserves—unnaturally small ranges, most often cages, where even the most inept hunters can take them as trophies, since the lions have no way of escaping. The notion of their genetic weakness has been disproved by the successful reintroduction of small numbers of white lions into the wild. Nevertheless, the canned hunting continues, and the white lions remain severely endangered.

The Zulu people believe that white lions are stars fallen to Earth, and they worship these lions as gods. The spiritual presence of all lions is powerful, and that of the white lions almost overwhelmingly so. For that reason, I found their message harder than most to render in human words. Though it reads a bit oddly, I have chosen to present it as it first came to me.

My energy and strength came to you combined with that of the two white lions—three of us [lioness energy] helped you enter deeper connection to the Source, to true courage and true power—this is most important for humans to gather now.

There is much confusion among humans of what real power is. Humans can confuse power [which is] that which comes from love, from the Source, confuse it with force—what you call bullets. Force causes sorrow and fear that will slow human development, human evolution. In this state courage is lost, when it is needed most.

One frozen in sorrow, fear, and loss of courage does not help lions, does not help humans. They weaken those who wish to be strong.

Know that when fear comes, the lion does not choose to run away. Fear gives us choice to invite in our courage, that which we all carry in abundance. It is always there for us. Unless it is given space to be, it remains unexplored, asleep. Courage must be released, cannot be held in a cage, as the great lions cannot be held in cages to wither and die, nor can any being.

In meditation with my sisters and with my brothers we helped you more clearly understand and experience lion connection to the Source and the harmony and reverence we share with all life in our kingdom. You have heard our sacred music— the sound of birds, the creatures, all life, carried by wind to our ears. Yes, we rule over our fellow beings throughout our sacred land. From only one group there are those who believe they are outside the kingdom—they are of the humans. This group of humans put themselves outside and have caused much damage to the kingdom that is sacred to us. Those who do not understand, or seek to exist in light.

There are many humans of course who we count among us—some in Africa, some in other lands. Not as strong as we in body but strong in heart, understanding courage and purpose. In our land, certain species are meant to outrun other species, but none of us can outrun the human bullets of force. White lions no longer have the chance to outrun bullets—we are born and raised in cages, no longer free to run. Those who have distorted nature's law, trying to claim lion courage and strength as their own by taking our body parts as prize—this is incorrect. This is not Source will. They are broken in the body part that is the mind. They try to gain from us by force what can never be possessed by force—that is true power. True power exists within nature's law—law of the Source. This idea "possession" is also not in nature. One cannot possess another; it is opposite to law. Nature shares and provides, but it is not possible to possess any being or land.

We lions have pride in the sacredness of life. All beings have place and purpose and all beings serve others in their way. Those whose bodies provide our food, our life are greatly honored by us. Many do not understand this. We are all parts within the one whole of Source. "God." The hunt for food for life is sacred to us—is Source serving Source. We take only what we require to live. We honor our kingdom. We honor life and death—also the sun and darkness—the old ones and the young—the dry days and the rains—the days of plenty and the days of hunger.

We reach out to the humans in our kingdom. It is time to hear, see, and feel the courage within your hearts. We send message of greeting. We do this by the blink of our eyes.

As you know, the eyes are links to heart and soul—the recognition of your sacredness. The landscape beyond the bush is the landscape of the Source, God's love. It is time to look there now. White lions are connected to other beings, working in the light, a sacred connection, with shaman and other keepers of the wisdom—they are now sharing our secrets, sometimes resulting in great hardship to them and those they love.

The name of our land, Timbavati, means "the place where the star lions come down" in human Zulu language. The Zulu shaman speaks of one called Queen Numbi, who lived on our land long ago. She bravely received us when her people saw a great light from the sky land nearby. We came, as you have heard, from star nations in the sky; we are beings of light. Queen Numbi carried on our story and sacred wisdom. This story of Queen Numbi is a way for you to understand what is difficult to understand.

We are beings of light, and the purpose of light is to shine and move freely, as we white lions once did in Timbavati. The light, love, and courage of white lion has purpose—to unite the Earth in God's light and love—honoring all beings, all nature, all life. What was once kept secret now belongs to all who will hear, hear with heart.

Our message is this: have faith in divine presence. We in spirit ask you to: take up your lion heart, your courage. Look at fear with strong, clear eyes. Do not look away. Rather, walk as lion does, toward fear. As you walk, with each step, the light will awaken stronger and stronger within you. You will feel us with you. We are with you in heart; we are with you in spirit. Strengthened by white-lion courage and consciousness of heart, work to unite the entire Kingdom so all beings may live in freedom and peace—a kingdom in which my brothers and sisters may roam the savanna once again.

Chapter 9

HEEDING THE CRIES
OF THE NONHUMAN WORLD

Not to hurt our humble brethren (the animals) is our first duty to them, but to stop there is not enough. We have a higher mission—to be of service to them whenever they require it.

—ST. FRANCIS OF ASSISI

Speak the voice in your heart and don't be afraid to make a lot of noise.

—LINDA BENDER

Animals remind us that all beings who walk, stand, swim, crawl, or fly are radiant, mysterious, and unique expressions of the Source. Every species, every culture has its own genius. Our human "species-specific genius"—our ability to protect and serve nature and the other beings with whom we share this world is desperately needed now. To see a problem and fix it utilizing our individual gifts that are alive in "the eye of your heart" is what the human heart aches to do.

Every day people are making a difference, creating change in their lives that positively impacts animals and nature. Change comes from dedicated, ordinary people, in the trenches, serving a cause greater than self.

The bald eagle has been our national symbol since 1782. The eagles were on the brink of extinction in 1973, and people spoke of the impending disappearance of this magnificent bird. From the 1930s to the 1960s, the combination of hunters, sheep ranchers, and DDT insecticide sprayed on crops decimated populations in the US and the birds became increasingly in danger of extinction. DDT, which was banned in the US in 1972, made its way through the food chain and caused eagle eggshells to become thin and the eggs to be sterile. The eagle was saved through the efforts of brave individuals who spent their Januaries tramping around the frozen Midwest looking for a single eagle's nest that remained. In Iowa, their hope was to save the eagle by finding and protecting any viable eggs they could locate in a nest, then incubating them. Even the most optimistic enthusiast could never have predicted the resiliency of the birds and the success of their comeback. In Iowa, environmentalists set a goal of ten or twenty nests by 2010. In 2011, federal staffers had lost count at 254 nests. The birds were removed from the endangered species list in 2007. Because of dedicated souls who marched through winter cold and snow, when we look up at the skies we can still see eagles. The eagles' return is a reminder of how a few dedicated people can change the future of a species, or an ecosystem.

Often in my conversations with people, they express feelings of helplessness saying "the problems are so overwhelming" and how can their efforts possibly make a difference? Each time we help one animal, we serve the greater good. Who can judge what one act of kindness will birth? Gandhi once said, "What you can do in response to the ocean of suffering may seem insignificant, but it is very important that you do it."

Listed here are simple things we can all do to improve the quality of our own lives, helping animals and our environment. Be creative and come up with your own list of ways to help.

- Be a voice for the voiceless; speak out against any injustice to animals you encounter.
- Recycle: when choosing packaged goods, select those with little or no plastic wrap.
- Pick up litter wherever you go, especially in or near water,

where litter can end up around the neck of a bird or embedded in a wing.

- Don't use plastic when you shop; carry tote bags. Plastic bags do not biodegrade, they break down into particles that contaminate the soil and water.
- Use less air conditioning in summer, less heat in winter.
- Do not spray pesticides and chemicals on lawns. Do not use bug zappers; they kill harmless insects that are food for birds, bats, etc.
- Read labels: do not buy products that use animals for testing and research.
- Teach children about nature through journeys and play in nature.
- Garden for wildlife, plant perennial gardens instead of grass. They attract birds, bees, and butterflies.
- Feed local birds. Remember in the winter to continue feeding as they will depend on you as a source of food. Feed until late spring.
- Provide water for wildlife, using birdbaths or small trays, especially in summer in developed area where natural sources of water are limited.
- Keep your cat indoors. Vulnerable native birds are prey. Some estimates say as many as five hundred million birds are lost each year to cats in North America.
- Adopt a pet, or donate your time or money to a shelter or animal sanctuary. Do not support puppy mills, or breeders, when millions of dogs and cats at shelters need homes.
- Do not buy animals taken from the wild and do not turn wildlife into pets.
- Do not buy products made from wild animals.
- If you see ivory or products made from wild animals in a store, make a point to tell the owner you will not shop there if he sells animal body parts.
- You can help native bees by buying or building a bumblebee house, wooden boxes designed for bees to nest.

- Build a bat house. Bats help humans by eating millions of flying insects—provide them a place to live.
- Plant trees. One tree can soak up as much as forty-eight pounds of carbon dioxide in one year and produce enough oxygen to sustain two human beings for life.
- Drive less, take public trains, and rideshare.
- When you travel, look into ecoconscious hotels that offer a variety of ways to "green" the travel experience. These hotels should be able to specify the ways in which they help and heal the planet.
- Drive slowly, observe speed limits. Remember, the roads we use have been cut through the habitats of wildlife. We share the roads with other beings.
- When driving or walking if you see an animal lost, in distress, or wounded, stop and help. Learn in advance which facilities in your area help animals in distress. If you rescue an animal you will know where to go.
- Protect, support, or help create local parks.
- We can become wildlife helpers when we join forces with other people. Everywhere I go, I meet individuals who work tirelessly in their communities to help animals—seek them out and help any way you can.
- Support organizations that are working to help animals and nature. More than ever, local animal shelters that give homeless companion animals a second chance at life need help. A few of my personal favorite organizations are Best Friends Animal Society; The Global White Lion Protection Trust (CEO Linda Tucker); The David Sheldrick Wildlife Trust, run by Daphne Sheldrick and her daughter Angela, who foster orphaned elephants and other animals and return them to the wild; The Center for Birds of Prey, located in Charleston, South Carolina (executive director James D. Elliott, Jr.); and Keeper of the Wild (director Janet Kinser) in St. George, South Carolina. Joining The

Sierra Club is a great way to stay connected to what is happening nationally, and they also have local branches around the country. The Wildlife Conservation Society is working especially hard to help the crisis of African elephant poaching. Other groups include The National Wildlife Federation, The League of Conservation Voters, World Wildlife Fund, or change.org on the Internet. Do your research; there are many wildlife/environmental nonprofit organizations to join, or start your own.

- Become a wildlife rehabilitator. Contact your State Fish and Game Agencies for licensing requirements. You can apprentice with someone already doing the job.
- Eat less (or no) meat. Read the book *Dominion*, by Matthew Scully. If you're eating meat, take a moment before each meal to honor the being who gave his or her life for you.
- Become a sacred activist. Read *The Hope*, by Andrew Harvey. Find what breaks your heart the most. That is where to begin.
- Meet or write to your mayor or other local representative. Act locally to stop the systematic destruction of local natural habitats.
- Maintain a daily prayer and meditation practice. Use the information in chapter seven to help.
- In order to maintain courage, clarity of purpose, and focus along your journey, write a simple poem or a prayer for yourself and recite it every day.

I share with you a prayer I wrote, which helps me stay in presence, in oneness, with all things:

Oh, Great Spirit
To better serve the animals,
In humble prayer I ask—
Show me what I need to see.

Teach me what I need to learn.
Show me truth.
Ignite my heart.
Transform my being, so that I may
Serve as a vehicle through which
Your voice flows out to the world,
Helping those who have no voice.

Afterword

We have a responsibility as human beings to be loving guardians and intimate, soulful companions to the amazing plethora of creatures that share life with us. We must awaken to the reverence for all life and create a call to action that protects and honors all life forms.

Animals of all kinds are uniquely equipped to teach us marvelous lessons and profound wisdom. By severing ourselves from nature and the great joy the love of animals gives us, we have become increasingly lonely on our gorgeous planet.

Loving our world deeply and tuning ourselves into the untamed intelligence of all living things enables us to find the passion, energy, and intuitive knowledge we now need in order to act urgently and wisely in every realm, to preserve the human race and protect what remains of God's nonhuman creatures and their habitats.

Linda Bender's wise, beautiful, poignant book is a huge contribution to our recovery from our long oblivion. She combines a scientist's clear understanding with a mystic's rapturous knowledge of the interconnection of all life and has a unique and simple way of communicating to us the many ways in which animals have enriched and informed her life.

Anyone who comes to this book will have his or her own understanding of animal beauty and wisdom immeasurably enriched and will be challenged gently to start becoming, as Linda is, a compassionate advocate for the animal kingdom and the natural world. This book will awaken within each one of us a wonder at creation, and our profound sacred responsibility to revere, cherish, and protect all living creatures in the name of a universal divine love that has created all things and lives in all things.

—Andrew Harvey
author of *The Hope: A Guide to Sacred Activism*

INDEX

A

Adam, story of, 5, 6
Aging, 108–9
Alexander, Charles, 23
Alexander, Eben, 119
Angels, communicating with, 36
Animal communicators, 129
Animals. *See also* Companion animals;
  Connecting with animals; *individual*
  animals
    aging and, 108
    anthropomorphizing, 147
    as bodhisattvas, 50–53
    children drawing pictures of, 7, 8
    compassion for, 47
    conception of time for, 70–71

concern of, for humans, 17–18, 62,
  152
consciousness of, 120
cultures of, 94–99
death and, 107, 118, 119–20, 122–25
effects of human population growth
  on, 16–17
emotions and, 136, 137
endangered species of, 14, 17, 151,
  161–62
ESP in, 22–25, 30–31
estrangement from, 6–7
for food, 9, 103–4, 165
gods depicted as, 8
grief and, 122–25
happiness of, 12–13, 15, 61, 69
in human-interest stories, 4–5

About the Author

Photo by Carolyn Evans

Linda Bender holds a doctorate degree in veterinary medicine and is a lifelong animal advocate. During the fourteen years she spent living in Europe, Asia, Africa, and the Middle East, her work included the rescue, rehabilitation, and protection of wildlife. Her interest in spirituality and healing led her to found the Mind the Gap Wellness Center as well as a pet therapy program. She is a certified meditation instructor and is a cofounder of the nonprofit organization From the Heart. Bender offers workshops and lectures worldwide on the relationship between humans, animals, and nature. Her website is lindabender.org.

SACRED ACTIVISM SERIES

When the joy of compassionate service is combined with the pragmatic drive to transform all existing economic, social, and political institutions, a radical divine force is born: Sacred Activism. The Sacred Activism Series, published by North Atlantic Books, presents leading voices that embody the tenets of Sacred Activism—compassion, service, and sacred consciousness—while addressing the crucial issues of our time and inspiring radical action.

Collapsing Consciously
Carolyn Baker

The More Beautiful World Our Hearts Know Is Possible
Charles Eisenstein

Earth Calling
Ellen Gunter
and Ted Carter

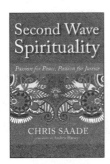

Second Wave Spirituality
Chris Saade

Pioneering the Possible
Scilla Elworthy
OCTOBER, 2014

Spiritual Democracy
Steven Herrmann
OCTOBER, 2014

The Sacred Activism Series was cocreated by Andrew Harvey, visionary, spiritual teacher, and founder of the Institute for Sacred Activism, and Douglas Reil, associate publisher and managing director of North Atlantic Books. Harvey serves as the series editor and drives outreach efforts worldwide.

For more information: www.nabcommunities.com/sacredactivism